General Editor: Gerald Moore

Wole Soyinka

Modern African Writers

Wole Soyinka

Gerald Moore

Africana Publishing Corporation · New York

Published in the United States of America 1971
by Africana Publishing Corporation
101 Fifth Avenue
New York, N.Y. 10003

Library of Congress Catalog Card No. 74–176321
ISBN 0-8419-0095-7
First published 1971

Photoset and printed in Malta by St Paul's Press Ltd.

Modern African Writers

Now that some of the initial excitement and misunderstanding surrounding African literature in English and French has begun to subside, it has become clear that it includes a small but growing number of writers who may be called 'serious'. I apply this word not simply to the tone of their books, but to the quality of their commitment to literature, to their sense of themselves as artists with a special and difficult role to fulfil, rather than just as people who happen to have published a book or two.

So much of the critical reception of this literature has been piece-meal, scattered and occasional that it isn't easy for the reader to determine who these writers are, what they have written, or what is the sequence and pattern of development of their work. In the present series, one volume will be devoted to each selected writer and will discuss his work critically, chronologically and consistently. In this way, the reader will be able to look at the writer's work as a developing whole or, if he prefers, turn to the chapter dealing with a particular book and see what the critic has to offer there. For one aim of this series is to reveal something about the present state of criticism in this field, as well as something about the work of its major writers.

No single school or method of criticism will be favoured in the selection of contributors to the series. Critics of this literature, both African and non-African, have themselves been subjected to influences as various as existentialism, négritude, structuralism and detailed textual analysis in the Anglo-American tradition; the series will doubtless reflect this variety of method and approach. Like-wise, the selection of authors to be studied will strive to reveal strength and interest wherever they exist, without enlisting itself for or against any particular movement. In this way, the series should enable itself to respond to every major development in African literature and criticism.

G. M.

Contents

The Author

Gerald Moore, M.A., is Reader in English in the School of African and Asian Studies at Sussex University. From 1953 to 1956 he lived and taught in various parts of Africa and the Far East. His major publications include *Seven African Writers*, *Modern Poetry from Africa* (with Ulli Beier), *The Chosen Tongue* and *Selected Poems of Tchacaya U Tam'si*. He has also contributed critical articles and translations to numerous books and journals in Africa, Europe and America.

Acknowledgments

The author wishes to acknowledge the kind assistance of Mr Wole Soyinka, who has read the manuscript and commented on several points of detail. Other assistance granted by Mrs Soyinka, Mr Wale Ogunyemi, Mr Segun Olusola, Mrs Peggy Harper and Mr Geoffrey Axworthy is gratefully acknowledged.

The author and publishers are also indebted to the following for permission to reproduce copyright material.

Associated Book Publishers and Hill and Wang for permission to reproduce extracts from 'Death of the Dawn', 'In Memory of Segun Awolowo', 'Easter', 'Abiku', 'Dedication', 'Post Mortem'. 'Prisoner', 'Harvest', 'Massacre', 'Malediction' and 'Idanre' from *Idanre and other Poems* by Wole Soyinka.

Curtis Brown and Harper and Row for permission to reproduce an extract from *Mister Johnson* by Joyce Cary.

Rex Collings for permission to quote extracts from *Poems from Prison* by Wole Soyinka.

André Deutsch and Collier Books for permission to reproduce an extract from *The Interpreters* by Wole Soyinka.

Epworth Press for permission to reproduce an extract from *West African Religion* by Geoffrey Parrinder.

Oxford University Press for permission to reproduce extracts from *The Swamp Dwellers*, *The Trials of Brother Jero*, *The Lion and the Jewel*, *A Dance of the Forests*, *The Strong Breed*, *The Road* and *Kongi's Harvest* from *Five Players*, *The Road*, and *Kongi's Harvest* by Wole Soyinka.

Routledge and Kegan Paul and Barnes and Noble for permission to reproduce an extract from 'The Fourth Stage' in *The Morality of Art*, ed. Jefferson.

The cover portrait of Wole Soyinka is reproduced by courtesy of *West Africa*.

The photographs of performances of *The Swamp Dwellers*, *The Lion and the Jewel* and *A Dance of the Forests* are reproduced by courtesy of Wole Soyinka.

The photograph of *The Road* is reproduced by courtesy of Douglas H. Jeffrey.

Where does one meet him?
One meets him in the place of battle;
One meets him in the place of wrangling:

There are seven Ogun who belong to me.

Introduction

The career of the Nigerian writer Wole Soyinka almost merits the hackneyed adjective 'meteoric'. Only 23 when his first plays were staged in London and Ibadan, he was recognized within a few years as the leading dramatist in Africa and one of the most talented at work anywhere in the English-speaking world. In the period 1960–7, Soyinka not only published and directed seven plays of his own but helped to launch in Nigeria the work of other black dramatists like Barry Reckord, Sarif Easmon and J. P. Clark. He wrote and directed two revues, formed two theatre companies, published an important novel and a fine volume of poems, contributed critical articles to numerous reviews, was a tireless controversialist and twice landed himself in jail.

Between his arrest by the Nigerian military authorities in August 1967 and his release in October 1969, a silence fell over all this ceaseless and various activity. For twenty-six months Soyinka was held virtually *incommunicado* and, at the time of writing, it is not clear what, beyond a couple of short poems, he was able to produce during this melancholy interlude. It seems probable, however, that it will always be seen as marking a definite break in his career, both as writer and as man of the theatre. The first decade of his activity is thus clearly marked off from whatever developments may now reveal themselves and, if justification is needed for offering a critical study of a writer who is still only thirty-six years old, it must lie therein.

Soyinka is not a man who often talks about his work in detail, or about the deepest experiences that have fed it. He combines a talent for society with an equally marked cultivation of solitude and silence. Yet so clearly is his work linked with certain events and experiences of his life that the critic cannot write of it, beyond the level of mere description, without making some attempt to associate the two. In the following pages, I have tried to preserve an association of this kind, relating each work to the author's total activity in the theatre and in society at the time of its conception.

Wole Soyinka was born at Abeokuta, Western Nigeria, in 1934. He is of the Yoruba-speaking peoples who populate most of Western Nigeria and the adjoining parts of Dahomey, his father being of the Ijebu group and his mother of the Egbas, who live in and around Abeokuta. This striking city, whose name means 'under the rock', lies astride the swift river Ogun which here flows through a wide bed full of great rounded boulders. Similar elephant-grey boulders cover the hills on which the city spreads and loom over it from the surrounding summits. Olumo Rock, which crowns one of these hills, was the shrine for the city's guardian deity and the scene of countless sacrifices in former days. Despite the teeming lorries and bicycles which fill the streets, or the festoon of electric and telephone cables overhead, Abeokuta still has a markedly traditional aspect and its dramatic site is a continual reminder of its pre-colonial origin as a federal capital for the Egbas, who gathered their strength here in the early nineteenth century and withstood terrible sieges by the Amazon armies of Dahomey.

The river Ogun, whose name links it with Soyinka's chosen deity, the Yoruba god of iron, war and craftsmanship, plays a central part in his novel *The Interpreters*. Amidst its waters the character called Egbo undergoes a physical experience of possession by the divine, and sees the huge boulders on which he is lying as the protruding toes of the god whose head lies far away at Olumo Rock. One of the master images of all his writing is a swift, rocky river-bed bridged by the striding and reckless road of man's modernity, or by the effort necessary to pass from one phase of existence to another. It may not be fanciful to relate these features of his work to the powerful impression made by Abeokuta's physical and spiritual presence upon the imagination of a boy growing up there.

After primary schooling in Abeokuta, Soyinka went to the Government College at Ibadan, capital of the then Western Region, which lies some 48 miles inland of Abeokuta. This was one of the leading secondary schools of Nigeria throughout the colonial period. After eighteen months working in the Government Medical Stores in Lagos, Soyinka won admission to the new University College of Ibadan in September 1952, at the age of eighteen. At this time there was no advanced level teaching available in Nigerian secondary schools. Entry to the University College was therefore at School Certificate level and undergraduates had to complete a two-year preliminary course there before entering on their degree work. The College had been open at Ibadan for just four years and already its students included Chinua Achebe and Christopher Okigbo, whilst John Pepper Clark, Michael Echeruo and Nkem Nwankwo also arrived at the college within the next few years. Such a concentration of literary talent was exceptional and did not recur after the early 'fifties. The reasons for it are a subject of speculation in Nigeria even today. It could be related to the fact that the opportunity to study language and literature to university standard was new to the country and exciting enough in itself. Again, the College then selected its students from all parts of Nigeria, taking only the best students from the leading secondary schools everywhere. The undergraduate society which resulted from this national selection was a new phenomenon in the society and existed within the context of a people awakening to consciousness of themselves, a people still hopeful and confident as they entered the final stages of the political struggle for independence.

Soyinka, however, remained in this atmosphere of nascent creativity for only two years, during which his histrionic flair found expression in starting a society of pirates. A photograph surviving from that period reveals a look of amused defiance in the tilted head of a swashbuckling young man, beneath his 'hirsuite hell chimney-spouts' of hair. At the end of this period, he removed to the School of English at Leeds University, where he took an honours degree in English in 1957. Leeds was at this time particularly active in university theatre, offering many productions of classical and modern European plays, often in their original languages.

Central to much of this activity was the figure of George Wilson Knight, whose position as one of Britain's most imaginative and controversial dramatic critics was already well established and whose writing was constantly informed by his experience as a Shakespearean actor and producer over some twenty-five years. To trace the precise lines of influence from one creative imagination to another always carries the dangers of literalism and pedantry, but it is noteworthy that in an important essay contributed to a volume recently presented to Wilson Knight[1], Soyinka has sought the meaning of tragedy for the Yoruba in terms of dramatic symbolism and 'the poetry of action', terms with which Knight himself has shown a life-long preoccupation. Knight's insistence in his criticism upon penetrating always to the structure of symbolism underlying dramatic ritual, whether in Shakespeare or in Ibsen, can safely be named as one of the strongest influences bearing upon Soyinka during these important years at Leeds, years during which his own swiftness and originality of mind seem to have impressed several of his teachers.

Soyinka himself did not begin writing for the stage at this time, but he was an assiduous playgoer and one who read widely in all the literature of the theatre. The three years of his studies at Leeds saw the writing of some of his early satirical poetry, such as 'The Other Immigrant', with its portrait of the sharply-dressed black student whose dignity is donned with his three-piece suit and who relishes the prospect of his return to the country 'where the one-eyed man is king'. The deflationary irony of this poem, its hatred of mirror-image imitation and social pretension, mark it as already a characteristic Soyinka product. But the light, scornful poetry published in *Black Orpheus* No. 5 in May 1959, the first of Soyinka's work to appear in Nigeria, gave no sign that a major tragic imagination was already in the making.

In the summer of 1957 Soyinka left Leeds after completing

---

[1] 'The Fourth Stage' in *The Morality of Art*, ed. D. W. Jefferson (Routledge and Kegan Paul, London, 1969).

his degree and began supply-teaching in London. It must have been during the course of the next year that he completed his first two plays, *The Swamp Dwellers* and *The Lion and the Jewel*, since both were ready for production by the summer of 1958. At this point Soyinka met Geoffrey Axworthy, who was teaching English at Ibadan and was looking for plays to produce at the new Arts Theatre there. Soyinka offered him the manuscripts of both plays for production at Ibadan. Meanwhile, he was himself preparing the first production of *The Swamp Dwellers*, which was presented at Student Movement House, London, in September 1958, as an entry for the University of London Drama Festival. In this production the part of Alu was played by Miss Francesca Pereira, a talented actress and singer who was later to be associated with a number of Soyinka's productions in Nigeria. The dramatist himself played the part of the rebellious son Igwezu.

During this time Soyinka's first marriage, to an English girl, took place and his first son was born. In the autumn of 1958 he began to work for the Royal Court Theatre in London as a script-reader, thereby acquiring the opportunity to watch the direction and stage-management of a number of plays at a time when the Court was very much the centre of the English dramatic revival. It was there, in the years between 1956 and 1960, that the early plays of John Osborne, Arnold Wesker, John Arden, Ann Jellicoe, Samuel Beckett and a number of other rising dramatists were first performed. Players like Joan Plowright, Mary Ure, Frank Finlay, Kenneth Haigh and Alan Bates all founded their reputations there during the same period. At the Royal Court Soyinka, who also joined their writers' group, was able to take part in presenting an evening of dramatic improvisation during the summer of 1959, whose cast included the newly-arrived South African actor Bloke Modisane and the West African Johnnie Saker, as well as Soyinka himself. The Hola Camp scandal of March that year provided material for one of the sketches, in which eleven Africans drank glasses of water and fell down dead, in eloquent

7

comment upon the original British account of the affair, which attributed all the deaths to a poisoned water-supply.

Later in the year, in a Sunday night presentation on 1 November, Soyinka presented a whole evening's entertainment with the title *The Invention and Other Tales*. In the first half of this programme he read a number of his poems, including the remarkable 'Telephone Conversation', which remains one of his most polished satirical achievements and one of the first fully mature poems to emerge from the new generation of Anglophone West African poets. 'Telephone Conversation' is very much a poem for recitation, timing its best effects in a way that is only fully evident when it is read to a waiting audience. Only some of that audience, however, seem to have appreciated its subtlety on this occasion and one critic actually found it 'crude'. This first part of the programme also included several poems sung to the guitar by Soyinka himself and several African musical items by other artists. The second part was devoted to Soyinka's one-act play, *The Invention*. This was inspired by an account he had heard of some of the scarcely-credible methods employed by the Nationalist Government of South Africa to detect the hidden 'natives' in their midst. The play imagines an American missile accidentally hitting South Africa in 1976, on the 200th anniversary of the Declaration of Independence. One particularly unwelcome effect of the explosion has been to rob the whole population of dark pigment, and it has become impossible to decide who is a 'native' and who is not. The first assignment given to the surviving scientists has been the solution of this problem, so that the familiar atmosphere of hatred, discrimination and segregation can be restored.

Critical reception of this play varied greatly. Most agreed that the idea was good, but many felt that Soyinka had been unable to develop it adroitly. Whereas Alan Brien in *The Spectator* found it reminiscent of 'an anti-white *die Sturme*', the *Jewish Chronicle* thought it 'a sadly witty play'. Most encouraging were *The Times* and *The Stage*. The critic of the former detected in Soyinka a morbid distrust of white audiences and a tendency to turn his back on them and mumble, but insisted that the ready response of the audience was due, not to a patronizing attitude towards his colour, but to 'respect for his gift for words'. *The Stage* found that:

> In his poems and songs Mr Soyinka has a true feeling for words and imagery and uses them fearlessly in all their richness; and he has a remarkably deep penetration of humanity and its motivation, coupled with a praiseworthy detachment and absence of axegrinding.

In the meantime the foundations of Soyinka's dramatic career in Nigeria itself had been laid, with the presentation at the Arts Theatre, Ibadan, of two of his early plays. On 20 and 21 February 1959 this theatre offered a double-bill of *The Swamp Dwellers* and *The Lion and the Jewel*, directed by Ken Post and Geoffrey Axworthy respectively. In *The Swamp Dwellers*, the part of the Blind Beggar was played by Dapo Adelugba, who was to be intimately associated with Soyinka's own theatrical enterprises in the following years. Another young student cast filled the leading roles in *The Lion and the Jewel*, with the future writer and critic Abiola Irele as Lakunle, the aspiring schoolmaster of this bucolic comedy.

These two highly successful productions were a revelation to the Nigerian audience. Here, only two years after the construction of the first proper theatre in the country, was an African dramatist who could people its stage with credible characters and fill their mouths with an English unmistakably local in its full-blooded ebullience. Clearly, Wole Soyinka must be brought home as soon as possible. And he himself, towards the end of his eighteen months with the Royal Court, was reaching the point where it was ever more necessary to end an absence of well over five years. The Rockefeller Foundation came up with a research fellowship in African traditional drama which would enable him to travel widely in Nigeria, studying and recording traditional festivals, rituals and masquerades rich in dramatic content. In the early months of 1960 Soyinka landed at Lagos with the early drafts of two new plays already in his pocket and a decade of intense creativity for the Nigerian theatre had begun.

I

Early Work in the Theatre

Although Soyinka's months at the Royal Court Theatre coincided with the English dramatic revival of the late 'fifties, it is unlikely that he felt much drawn to the actual products of that revival; the intense Utopianism of Wesker's trilogy,[1] for instance, or the egomaniac heroes of John Osborne, locked in their obsessions with a highly-selective personal past. John Arden, a writer of infinitely greater dramatic resource and of strong, fastidious prose, may have had more to offer him by reason of the very eclecticism of his own influences. But the most fruitful aspect of those months, apart from the opportunity to make one of his own early essays in production, is likely to have been the phenomenon of the Court itself, proving once more the enduring vitality of the theatre and its ability to command the mood and idiom of a new generation.

Suddenly it was again conceivable for a young man or woman of intellect and sensitivity to seek a career in the theatre rather than as novelist, poet or critic. The greater profitability of the choice became apparent more gradually, as the first wave of dramatists emerged as substantial men of business in the film world, but no doubt the obvious glamour of first nights and long runs contributed its attraction from the first. A young novelist may hear the work of years launched with a little plop into the great indifferent sea of the month's new books. Anxiously he awaits the few, pitifully inadequate reviews he may be lucky enough to get. The dramatist who is able to get his play on to the stage at all has the opportunity to assist in the imaginative realization of his work from the text and then

---

[1] *Chicken Soup with Barley, Roots,* and *I'm Talking About Jerusalem.*

to witness night after night the actual process of its communication to a diverse, constantly varying audience. Despite the paraphernalia of dinner-jackets, chandeliers and cocktails which sometimes accompanies it, the theatre is still the most primitive in its immediacy of all our means of organized communication. It is man speaking to men, without the interposition of canvas, microphone, camera or the printed page. Its potentialities for a society already accustomed to the ritual speech, mime and movement of the ceremonial occasion; already receptive to the transformations of personality wrought by costume, masquerade and vocal projection, would need no labouring for a young African writer eagerly making links between his distant people and his foreign, elitist education. Furthermore, drama has unique capacities for social unification, in that it works through the eye and the spoken word. Hence, if rightly shaped and performed, it can be equally accessible to literate and illiterate, to the educated Christian convert and the traditionalist, or, in Elizabethan terms, to the stagebox and the groundlings. Add the means of dissemination offered by radio and television to those already explored by the itinerant troupe, and the advantages of drama over all other literary means of expression in contemporary Africa are seen to be decisive.

Soyinka would have needed no convincing of the error of those who argued that drama was 'new' to Africa. Only ignorance of the real origins and nature of drama could encourage such an opinion. Pierre Verger's description and photographic record of the Ogun ceremonies regularly performed in the Yoruba villages of Ishede and Ilodo, both situated in south-eastern Dahomey, evoke the power, beauty and reverence with which his worship is constantly celebrated and renewed. The villagers dance, sing and act out their dependence upon Ogun, god of iron, war and hunting, every week of their lives.[1] The whole population of Ilodo waits breathless as the flickering flame, carried by the one-legged imp Aroni, comes out

---

[1] *Les Dieux d'Afrique*, Pierre Verger (Hartmann, Paris, 1954), pp. 78–90 and 179–82.

of the darkness of the forest to kindle their extinguished hearths and to renew the divine contract which guarantees the activities of hunter, warrior and smith. The motif of seasonal death and resurrection which is so strongly rooted in the Dionysian cult, and hence in the Greek tragedies which grew directly out of it, could find no stronger ritual expression than that recorded by Geoffrey Parrinder for the reception of initiates to the 'convents' of Sango and Sakpata among the Fon and the Sha-Yoruba of the Dahomey-Nigeria border regions. Here is a ritual which shows the fullest possible use of dramatically expressive action, in which everyone is involved and everyone must play a part, but in which the initiates themselves are kept constantly involved with their role. A tribal spectator, or even a parent, might turn aside for a moment to chat, to chew groundnuts or to swill palm-wine, but the initiate cannot step out of a role in which he is held alike by the tradition, by the expectations of the audience, and by his own expectation of experiencing a genuine change of personality:

> The dance is held on the open space in front of the convent. The door of the convent is covered with a mat, red, white, and black. In front are the stools of the priests. A goat is sacrificed early in the morning, and the blood sprinkled on the principal shrine ... When the drums begin, a crowd quickly gathers, and the devotees come out of the convent and begin to dance ...
>
> The secretly designated candidate soon cries out and works his way through the excited crowd into the midst of the dancers, where he begins to twirl wildly. He dances ever more furiously until he falls stark on the ground, as in an epileptic fit. The dancers, after circling round the 'corpse', wrap it in a shroud and, singing dirges, carry it into the convent.
>
> The laity believe that the neophyte has actually died[1] ... Once in the convent, the shroud is undone, and drink is given.

---

[1] This is very hard to assess, as it would be sacrilege to deny this belief, just as it would be to say that a masked dancer is 'really old so-and-so'. It is quite possible that the laity fully appreciate that the death and resurrection are symbolic of the end of the initiate's old life and the beginning of a new one.

The novice is instructed in his future role and how to act. Each night for seven nights he sleeps in his shroud. A goat is killed, and its blood and skin reserved for later use. On the evening of the seventh day, the wrapped body is borne into the temple, and the body smeared with 'medicine'. Songs are sung round the 'corpse', and the parents may be allowed to assist at this ceremony.

On the eighth day is held the ceremony of 'resurrection'. The neophyte is held by outsiders to have been dead since the week before, and now to be raised by the power of the god. The usual preliminaries of sacrifice precede dancing in the public place.

The supposed corpse is then carried out of the convent by acolytes. It is wrapped in reed mats as for a funeral and smells abominably, because wrapped in with it is the skin of the goat or fowl which was killed the week before. Women kneel by the corpse, sprinkle it with water, and fan away flies.

The priest then comes forward and, kneeling by the 'corpse' he calls upon the god for help to restore the dead one to life. Seven times he calls upon the 'deceased' by name, and it is not till the seventh time, when the relatives begin to get anxious, that the body gives a grunt. The others then press round and unfasten the grave clothes. They lift up the neophyte, whose body is daubed with red and white. With their aid he staggers seven times round the drums, and is then led into the convent to begin his training and become a new being, to the thunderous applause of the excited crowd . . .

The novice is now called a prisoner of the war, since the god has captured him from his family. The duty of the family is now to bring presents of food to the convent. Except on the morrow, they will not see their relative any more until the end of his monastic seclusion, but they must provide for his material needs.[1]

Parrinder goes on to explain that this seclusion formerly lasted some three years, though the demands of colonialism for manpower led to its reduction to nine months for boys. At the

---

[1] *West African Religion*, Geoffrey Parrinder (Epworth, London, 1949), pp. 94–5.

end of it, the initiate will be found to have changed his name and to speak a new language, taught only in the convent. Anyone carelessly calling him by his old name commits a serious taboo.

Quite apart from the light this ritual sheds upon the affair of Christ and Lazarus, it will be seen that any touring company bringing a play to a community of this kind is scarcely likely to find that the ideas of dramatic enactment or of total involvement in a role are new. If the play is based upon a theme or situation already familiar to the audience, it will command attention and participation of a kind seldom found in the 'entertainment' theatre of the West.

Another example may be taken from Nigeria itself, where the cult of the dead known as Egungun surrounds the death of one of its members with a ritual designed to show both the immortality of his spirit and the special character of his membership, now that he is no longer 'the mask of the ancestors', but an ancestor himself. On the seventh day after the death of the husband, the widows are led out of town by a masked Egungun to a clearing where mounds of earth have been heaped up to the number of the surviving wives. Each mound has a yam on it, which is taken by the widow as the last gift of her husband. But there is one additional mound with no yams, representing the dead man himself. After another week, a masked Egungun comes to the house by night. The lights are put out and he calls upon the dead man. Another Egungun, concealed behind the house, replies in the voice of the deceased. Amid lamentations a dog is sacrificed and carried away. Next morning the masked Egungun returns as the dead man to give last blessings to his family and receive presents. The Egungun members then repair to their forest grove to eat the dog. Thus every stage in the gradual withdrawal of the dead man's presence and spirit from the intimacy of the household to the After-life is clearly marked by a dramatic ritual involving both the secret society and the family.

It is reasonable to hazard a guess that many rituals and ceremonies of this nature were in Soyinka's mind as he prepared to return to Nigeria and began work upon his first major play, *A Dance of the Forests*. In the meantime, he wasted no time in involving himself with the new possibilities opened up by the existence of a well-equipped theatre at Ibadan and of a rapidly-growing group of young people with a strong commitment to dramatic work. Within a few months of his arrival he played a leading role in Brecht's *Caucasian Chalk Circle*, directed by Geoffrey Axworthy at the Arts Theatre. During these first few months he also completed the manuscript of his third play, the one-act farce *The Trials of Brother Jero*, which was first produced by an Ibadan student group in the late spring of 1960, again at the Arts Theatre, with Remi Adeleye as the Prophet Jeroboam.

By May 1960 Soyinka had completed the first part of *A Dance of the Forests* and had formed his first acting company, *The 1960 Masks*. This consisted mainly of young graduates who had begun working in such fields as television, broadcasting, journalism and teaching. Drawing his cast partly from Ibadan and partly from Lagos, Soyinka was obliged to travel constantly on the treacherous 90-mile road between the two cities, often rehearsing in the back of his Landrover as it hurtled through the darkness. The gestation of his poem 'Death in the Dawn' and of his subsequent tragedy *The Road* may well be sought in the experiences of this time. In five hectic months the play was finished, rehearsed and got ready for production at the Nigerian Independence Celebrations on 1 October 1960. It also won the prize offered by the British monthly review *Encounter* to mark the occasion. This was a large-scale, elaborate and extremely demanding production, calling for highly-rehearsed singing, dancing and masquerading fully interwoven with the verbal texture of the play. And, in addition to directing his large company, Soyinka himself undertook the important part of Forest Father. In less than a year he had achieved a position of dominance in the unfolding theatrical scene of Nigeria. Before turning to examine *A Dance of the Forests*, let us look in some detail at the three plays written and produced by the time he was twenty-five.

This is the least substantial of Soyinka's plays, although it may well 'work' better on the stage than *A Dance of the Forests*. It exhibits a surface of prose realism, with none of the extra devices that Soyinka usually employs to enrich his dramatic texture, ranging from verse and song to dance, masquerade and pantomime. Only the Drummer and the little procession of the Kadiye briefly disturb this prosaic texture. The play's somewhat grim surface is, however, heavy with a symbolic meaning which extends beyond its apparent theme of rural decay. The immediate impression is of a play of gloomy peasant realism in the manner of Gerhard Hauptmann. The action is set at nightfall in a simple hut that stands among the swamps of a riverine district suggesting the Niger Delta. A quarrelsome old couple, Makuri and his wife Alu, are awaiting the return of their son Igwezu, who has gone out to visit his flooded farm nearby. Out of the darkness three arrivals come to them in succession, each serving to illuminate their situation and ring changes upon the themes of drought and flood, dearth and plenty, impatience and humility.

The first to enter is a Blind Beggar who has walked all the way from the North, following the long river from a land of perpetual drouth and locusts until he finds one where the soil is always moist. But he finds Makuri's household staggering under the weight of an opposite misfortune, for here the river has flooded and destroyed many farms. There is also much good land unused in these parts, for it is sacred to 'The Serpent of the Swamps' and no-one may cultivate it. Their next visitor is the Kadiye, Chief Priest to the Serpent of the Swamps and the villagers' only safeguard against the vagaries of the river. It is to the Kadiye that they must make an annual offering from their produce so that the holy Serpent may spare their crops. The Kadiye is consoling, plausible and fat. Finally comes Igwezu himself, raging with bitterness against the Kadiye who has deceived him, against the city where his elder brother has robbed him of money and wife, against the land which has despoiled his final hopes as a returning prodigal son. Yet the

Beggar discerns a kind of strength in this angry youth who blames everyone but himself for his misfortunes. He offers to serve Igwezu and to fructify his fields with those dry toes and fingers which so long for the embrace of mud. Igwezu accepts his service offhandedly, but remains intent upon his vendetta against the Kadiye, who he now sets down for an over-fed rascal and an obstacle to all advancement in the area. Makuri and Igwezu being the local barbers, the Kadiye has come for a shave, for he predicts an imminent break in the long rains which will release him from his onerous vow to remain unshaven as long as they last. While he sits helpless in the chair, Igwezu menaces him with the open razor:

IGWEZU: You lie upon the land, Kadiye, and choke it in the folds of a serpent.

MAKURI: Son, listen to me . . .

IGWEZU: If I slew the fatted calf, Kadiye, do you think the land might breathe again? If I slew all the cattle in the land and sacrificed every measure of goodness, would it make any difference to our lives, Kadiye? Would it make any difference to our fates?

KADIYE: (*in a choking voice*) Makuri, speak to your son . . .

BEGGAR: Master . . . Master . . .

> (*Igwezu suddenly shaves off the final smear of lather with a rapid stroke which makes the Kadiye flinch. Releases him and throws the razor on the table. Kadiye scrambles up at once, tearing the cloth from his neck. Makes for the door.*)

KADIYE: (*panting*) You shall pay for this . . . I swear I shall make you pay for this . . .[1]

The melodramatic flatness of the Kadiye's response here is a fair example of what is weakest in the play. The language generally lacks Soyinka's usual distinction and energy, though here and there it achieves a certain brooding strength. It is partly the failure to realize the Kadiye as a person which accounts for the weakness of his lines; he is a stage villain,

---

[1] *Five Plays* by Wole Soyinka (Oxford University Press, 1964), p. 195.

although Igwezu's case against him is a bad one if it rests only on his failure to deliver good harvests every year. Neither faith nor science can promise that.

The play ends with Igwezu rushing angrily off to the city again, though as the land is dark and flooded there is more likelihood of his finding death than fulfilment. Brushing aside the Beggar's remonstrances, he says:

> Only the children and the old stay here, bondsman. Only the innocent and the dotards.[1]

Alu and Makuri having already left the stage, only the Beggar remains as the lights fade and he mutters:

> I shall be here to give account.[2]

Soyinka has shown us a pagan rural community which is disintegrating because the young, unable to accept poverty and hazard, no longer have faith in its life or its narrow gods. For them the attraction of the city is as much negative as positive; it is a way of getting off the land. If the city destroys every obligation of kinship and friendship, as Igwezu has already learnt, it also destroys the kind of sanctified exploitation represented by the Kadiye. On the land, even the old have become querulous and sad, grieving for their lost children and turning their resentment against each other. Whence, then, does the Beggar draw the quiet dignity and faith which distinguish him in the play? It is not enough to reply simply 'from Islam', for although Soyinka in this play seems intent on showing us a bankrupt paganism, he is most unlikely to follow this up with a Muslim encomium. The real secret of the Beggar's strength is surely that his demands are minimal. While Igwezu flees the land because it does not produce for someone who has effectively already abandoned it (for he has been long in the city when the play opens), the Beggar is confident that his love and need for it will make it yield. He does not need the Kadiye

---

[1] *Ibid.*, p. 197.   [2] *Ibid.*, p. 198.

to stand between him and misfortune. Having known blindness, destitution and drought all his life, he senses the promise of a harvest where the others see only bitterness and failure.

It is perhaps the characterization of the Blind Beggar which makes this play vaguely reminiscent of J. M. Synge's rural comedies. In Synge's *The Shadow of the Glen*, an unknown Tramp likewise erupts upon the lonely lives of Dan and Nora Burke as night is falling. And *The Well of the Saints* actually offers us a Blind Beggar (also a sacred figure in Yeatsian mythology) in the person of Martin Doul, who finally rejects the gift of sight and pursues his own proud and separate way. It is natural that the example of Synge should have appealed to another poet seeking to bring into dramatic literature in English the life of an alien people whose culture, language, fundamental values and rhythm of life differ radically from those predominant in English drama itself since 1660. And like Synge before him, Soyinka is already striving for an arrangement of English which, whilst comprehensible to all users of that tongue, will continually suggest another language, another world of sounds, lying beyond it.

THE COMEDIES

Few of Soyinka's plays fit neatly into the classical dramatic categories. To some extent this is true of much modern Western drama also, and the convenient but somewhat loose category of 'tragi-comedy' has been extended by critics to cover plays ranging from Ibsen's *Wild Duck* to Brecht's *Threepenny Opera*. How, for instance, are we to classify a play like *A Dance of the Forests*? Its basic form is that of classical comedy, very close to such 'transformation and restoration' plays as *A Midsummer Night's Dream* or *As You Like It*. A group of characters are shown to us as estranged from themselves and in some disharmony, open or subdued, with each other. In a long central section they are led into the disorienting world of the forest, where they are played upon by unsuspected forces which bring them to some recognition of themselves and their proper destinies. The last act shows the restoration of these characters to their normal world, with the prospect of a new and richer life ahead for some of them, at least. Yet, unlike these Shakespearean examples, the prevailing tone of Soyinka's play is far from comic. It is filled with a sense of the repetitive futility, folly and waste of human history. Even the play's last lines are dark with new meanings, and there is no roseate glow of restored love and harmony cast over the stage by the dramatist.

Similarly, *The Swamp Dwellers* refuses all convenient categories, for it offers only a mock *agon* and no death, despite its somewhat gloomy and foreboding atmosphere. But in *The Lion and the Jewel* Soyinka has written an almost classical comedy of village life, even if his moral is challengingly unconventional. And *The Trials of Brother Jero* may be described without violence to its character as a satirical farce. It is the easiest, shortest, funniest and probably the most frequently produced of Soyinka's seven published plays.

(i) The Trials of Brother Jero

Brother Jeroboam is a religious charlatan of a type particularly common in societies where traditional faith is collapsing but where the illiterate populace retains a deep need for apocalyptic, self-annihilating frenzy, for simple slogans of salvation and for public ritual. The Bar Beach at Lagos has long been a favoured resort for various break-away churches and religious eccentrics who fuse elements of Christianity and African paganism into creeds of their own. Such creeds usually accomodate the demand of their worshippers to unite singing, drumming, clapping and dancing into a single act of praise. They allow room for trances, possession and 'speaking with tongues' among the congregation. They offer to their faithful supporters the twin attractions of success in this world and salvation in the next.

Such a 'church' is Brother Jero's and, although his disciples appear to be few, they suffice to give him a simple living. The play makes use of blackouts, pools of light on a darkened stage and a simple scene-change to show us all the dodges and evasions he needs to practise in a single day to keep himself in business. Soyinka's satire upon his rogueries is genial rather than fierce; his abundant energy and resource make it seem right as well as inevitable that he should triumph over every adversity. And, in the manner of such classical rogues as the Jew of Malta or Scapin, he invites the audience to share in the enjoyment of his ingenuity. Thus, in the first of five short scenes we see Brother Jero exulting in his own skill, telling the audience about his former knavery in outwitting the Old Prophet who once taught him his trade, and complaining of declining congregations in these days of television and high-life. The Old Prophet has, however, cursed him to be undone by the Daughters of Discord and we see in the action he presents to us that women always offer the chief threat to his security and peace of mind. The shrew Amope, to whom he owes money for all the goods he has got on credit, is harder to outwit than her long-suffering husband Chume, his principal disciple. And the drowsy girl who flaunts herself before him every morning always shatters his carefully-built façade of austerity and other-worldliness. But in the end he outsmarts them all, though he is reduced to having an enraged Chume taken off by the police on a charge of assault.

The play presents Soyinka's first use of pidgin English, which was to assume such importance in *The Road*. Here Chume takes over the congregation while Brother Jero goes in pursuit of an irresistible Daughter of Discord. Beginning in a panic attempt to pacify a frantic penitent, Chume's prayers gradually take on the form and rhythm of a splendid fantasy, offering material success to both emperor and clown:

CHUME: Father, forgive her.
CONGREGATION: Amen.
CHUME: I say make you forgive 'am.
CONGREGATION: Amen.
CHUME: Forgive 'am one time.
CONGREGATION: Amen.
CHUME: Forgive 'am quick quick.
CONGREGATION: Amen.
CHUME: Yes, Father, make you forgive us all. Make you save us from palaver. Save us from

trouble at home . . . Give us money to satisfy our daily necessities. Make you not forget those of us who dey struggle daily. Those who be clerk today, make them Chief Clerk tomorrow. Those who are Messenger today, make them Senior Service tomorrow . . . (*the Amens of the congregation grow more and more ecstatic*).

Those who are petty trader today, make them big contractor tomorrow. Those who dey sweep street today, give them their own office tomorrow. If we dey walka today, give us our own bicycle tomorrow . . . Those who have bicycle today, they will ride their own car tomorrow. (*The enthusiasm of the response becomes overpowering*) I say those who push bicycle today, give them big car tomorrow. Give them big car tomorrow. Give them big car tomorrow . . .[1]

Here Soyinka's ear is still not completely sure in its shaping of pidgin dialogue (for instance, the ponderous 'satisfy our daily necessities' and the unlikely circumlocution, 'those of us who'), but Chume's gradual slide into more and more ecstatic exclamations attuned to the real desires of his hearers is an adroit use of pidgin as part of the verbal texture of the play, nicely placing Chume's 'no nonsense' attitude towards religious observance.

This slight but effective work has one structural weakness, at the beginning of Scene Five. Here Jero is about to win the allegiance of an M.P. by posing as a messenger of God bringing him news of a Ministerial appointment, but the speech which the M.P. is practising when Jero disturbs him is indicated only as a mime. In the 1966 production of this play by Atholl Fugard at the Hampstead Theatre Club a comic speech was specially written for the M.P. to open the scene with, and this undoubtedly improved its effectiveness as a whole. At the end of the play, the M.P. prostrates himself at the feet of the

[1] *Ibid.*, pp. 218–20.

supposedly divine Brother Jero with a cry of 'Master!' And we are obliged, in a sense, to agree with his estimation of a memorable rogue.

(ii) The Lion and the Jewel

The originality of Soyinka's rural comedy lies in two things; firstly, the great scope which he allows here for mime and for dramatically expressive dance and movement; secondly, the deliberately provocative moral of the ending, which reverses the assumption of so much culture-conflict literature that the heroine must always plump for 'progress' and 'enlightenment'. It was this latter aspect of the play which caused one leading London critic to dub it 'reactionary', not recognizing that one of the first duties of the comedian is the exploding of *cliché*. In other respects, the structure of the play is more conventional than that of his other three full-length works: *A Dance of the Forests*, *The Road* and *Kongi's Harvest*. His usual concern with liberating his action from the limits of a single 'line' in space and time here finds only muted expression, for Soyinka is rightly intent upon keeping his comic plot moving along a single plane of reality. He even obeys the classical 'unities' since, as in most of his plays, he confines his action to a single place and a single day. But the scene in 'Morning' (the first act) where Sidi and her friends force Lakunle to mime the role of the visiting photographer is an economic and effective device, for it not only recreates for us the original comedy of the white man's arrival in the village, but it presents Lakunle with his best opportunity in the play for gaining some of the audience's sympathy. In the hands of a good actor, Lakunle thus becomes something more than a gawky figure of ridicule and a butt for the whole community. We should feel for him, even if we are obliged to endorse Sidi's final preference for the old Lion of Ilujinle. It is also a splendid miming, dancing and drumming opportunity for the entire cast, and a notable 'warmer-up' for the play at an important point in its development.

The arrival of the Bale in the middle of this scene is given a naturalistic explanation; although he arrives 'right on cue', we can assume if we wish that he has been hovering in the vicinity in order to do so. But in 'Noon' we have another mimed re-enactment in which Soyinka departs much farther from the conventions of naturalistic comedy. Lakunle begins reminiscing about the Bale's cunning in staving off the injurious effects of 'progress', as instanced in his deflection of the railway away from his village in the old days. Immediately the stage actually becomes that scene of ancient villainy. The contemporary players, Lakunle, Sidi and Sadiku, withdraw from the action and are replaced by actors miming the encounter between the Bale and the advancing railway-workers long ago. The technique here has something in common with the stage musical, where similar suspensions of natural action are accepted as part of the convention. It is another example of Soyinka's freedom, right from the start of his career, in the choice of theatrical means that he employs. This second passage of mime does not perform as many functions as the first, but it does increase the general fluidity of the action and extend it momentarily beyond the normal limits of one-dimensional comedy. It also dramatizes Baroka's ability to come to terms with encroaching modernity and exploit it for his own ends, as he does later in his handling of Sidi.

For the rest, Soyinka depends upon the imaginative life he is able to bestow upon his principal characters. Further to differentiate Sidi, Lakunle and Baroka from the lay figures of the plot, he gives them a loose, unrhymed verse of shortish lines for all their speeches. This was Soyinka's first attempt to use verse in the theatre and he does not entirely master the special problems which it poses. Lacking the charged intensity of tragic speech, a verse comedy seems to demand some special quality of wit, precision or balance to justify itself. Shakespeare provides this with his powerful lyricism and almost unfailing rhythmic control, Molière with the continual 'point' and perfectly timed surprise of his rhyming couplets; but there are many Elizabethan comedies, such as Thomas Dekker's, in which the use of verse seems purely conventional. Rejecting most of the technical devices which might lend precision to his speech, Soyinka can depend only on the constant felicity of his ideas to maintain the poetic content of his lines. Often the mere printing as poetry appears to contribute nothing to the effect of the speech. Lakunle poses special difficulties in this respect, because the 'corny' and derivative nature of his ideas makes for bathos in itself and might be more effectively satirized in prose. Only the fervour of his conviction may justify the use of poetry here:

> I want to walk beside you in the street
> Side by side and arm in arm
> Just like the Lagos couples I have seen
> High-heeled shoes for the lady, red paint
> On her lips. And her hair is stretched
> Like a magazine photo. I will teach you
> The waltz and we'll both learn the foxtrot
> And we'll spend the weekend in night-clubs at Ibadan.[1]

The language here is at least appropriate to the sort of 'decent' petitbourgeois preoccupations Lakunle represents. We can imagine him putting lace-doyleys on every horizontal surface in his house and promoting dances in which African costume, 'knickers' and palm-wine are alike prohibited. But occasionally his speeches also show a disturbing archaism and literary heaviness which is not consistent with these *Drum*-derived[2] ideas:

> I know him what he is. This is
> Divine justice that a mere woman
> Should outstrip him in the end.[3]

We cannot be certain whether the Shakespearean echoes here (cf. Prince Hal's, 'I know you what you are' in *Henry IV, Part* 1) contribute to the effect Soyinka intends or merely injure it. They are certainly at variance with the general pattern of Lakunle's language, which springs more from a diet of

---

[1] *Ibid.*, pp. 100–1.

[2] *Drum* is a popular African weekly, originating in Johannesburg, whose advertisements and features equally promote Westernized tastes and values in make-up, hairstyles, dress, furnishings and ways of life.

[3] *Five Plays*, p. 104.

magazines, newspapers and dictionaries than directly from Eng. Lit.

But these difficulties are admittedly at their most acute in the part of Lakunle. Sadiku and Sidi attempt fewer 'flights'; the malicious cunning of the old woman and the excited flirtatiousness of the girl come through well enough and there is only an occasional false note, such as Sidi's awkwardly literary remark on first seeing the Bale's stamping-machine in the palace:

> I have never seen the like.[1]

Sadiku's part, being written in prose throughout, is free from the sort of strain which produces lines like these. Not so Baroka's which, although full of delightful touches and nice opportunities for comic timing, also betrays a literary quality from time to time:

> What an ill-tempered man I daily grow
> Towards. Soon my voice will be
> The sand between two grinding stones.
> But I have my scattered kindliness
> Though few occasions serve to herald it.[2]

Examples like these serve to show that Soyinka had not yet fully mastered the problem of hammering out an acceptable English diction for an African poetic drama which, though constantly referring itself to tradition, would be contemporary in flavour. In *A Dance of the Forests* it is the metaphysical complexity of Forest Father's message which causes an occasional wordiness of language:

> CRIER: Only such may gain
> Voice auditorial as are summoned when their link
> With the living has fully repeated its nature, has
> Reimpressed fully on the tapestry of Igbehinadun
> In approximate duplicate of actions, be they
> Of good, or of evil, of violence or of carelessness;

---

[1] *Ibid.*, p. 142.

[2] *Ibid.*, p. 139.

> In approximate duplicate of motives, be they
> Illusory, tangible, commendable or damnable.[1]

As a fleeting clue to a theatre audience, this could scarcely be more impenetrable. *The Lion and the Jewel* has no such complexities to wrestle with and its occasional failures of language spring only from the tension between poetic and prosaic qualities within the play itself. It remains, despite these, a play of exceptional charm and dexterity. A production such as Atholl Fugard's, at the Hampstead Theatre Club in 1966, brought out these qualities to the full. Femi Euba's gawky appeal and genuine feeling gave to the part of Lakunle a perfect balance of satire and sympathy, while Jumoke Debayo's sidling stance and mischievous, wheedling voice gave Sadiku all the physical reality of a great comic character. The comic plot is well-balanced and adroitly handled, with a constant shift of sympathy from one character to another. We come to see that Baroka is no mere stereotyped reactionary. It suits his character and position to keep modern influences at arm's length, but his seduction of Sidi by means of the stamping-machine and magazine photographs show that he is well able to make those influences work for his own convenience. He is far more secure in such dealings than Lakunle, whose pretended contempt for the village is partly a compensation for his lack of wealth, strength or good looks, just as his moral refusal to pay bride-price is rooted in his inability to do so. Lakunle's claims to sophistication will scarcely prevent his being dismissed as a 'bushman' when he reaches the city. This is the pitiful part of his dilemma and, in a well-judged performance of the role, his strongest claim upon some of the audience's final sympathy.

It will be seen that *The Lion and the Jewel* handles some of the same material as *The Swamp Dwellers*, but Soyinka's touch here is not only lighter, it is also surer. Baroka is far more shrewdly observed and dramatically interesting than the somewhat inert figure of the Kadiye, and Lakunle is a more

---

[1] *Ibid.*, p. 50.

memorable example of someone at home in neither country nor city than the bitter, unvaried character of Igwezu. The obvious merits of *The Lion and the Jewel* as a stage comedy have led to its becoming one of the most popular of all Soyinka's plays. In Nigeria itself, its first production has been followed by several others, and it has also been presented in many other parts of Africa, in London, in the United States and as far away as New Guinea.

2

A Dance of the Forests

The first performance of *A Dance of the Forests* was also the first announcement of Soyinka's tragic imagination, his severely circumscribed hopes for what African independence might achieve, and the demands which he was now prepared to make upon the comprehension of his audience. If more people had understood the play's implications in 1960, it is likely that there would have been an outcry against the author's sober expectations of his countrymen, as well as against his obscurity. Nonetheless, those who had genuine hopes of the African theatre could not fail to be stimulated by the appearance of a work of such scale and ambition. Soyinka's potentialities as a writer were clearly extended far beyond anything that his earlier plays and poetry might suggest.

The play opened at Yaba Technical College, Lagos, in October 1960 and was shortly afterwards transferred to the Arts Theatre at Ibadan University. This, so far as I can ascertain, is the only production of *A Dance of the Forests* to date and it was Soyinka's first opportunity to involve himself closely in the realization of one of his plays in African conditions. The sets and costumes for the play were designed by the young Nigerian artist Demas Nwoko, who has since been much absorbed with theatre design at Ibadan. The double role of Obaneji/Forest Father was played by Soyinka himself and the small parts of the Sweeper, Dirge-Man and others by Femi Euba, who was later to become a well-known professional actor in London. Several other actors in the cast-list, notably Yemi Lijadu and Ralph Okpara, were to be associated with many of Soyinka's productions in the coming years.

In writing the play itself, Soyinka must clearly have spent much thought on devising the means for his characters' disorientation from their workaday selves and the glimpse of self-knowledge which this makes possible. An African dramatist would have to reach no farther than the nearest grove to find examples of the forest as the great theatre where changes in the state of being are enacted. There dwells Osanyin, god of medicine and occult knowledge; there the Egungun, Oro, Agemo and many other secret cults hold their meetings; and there goes every initiate, whether at puberty or later in life, who seeks to lose his old self and discover another. In modern Nigeria, as in medieval England and colonial America, the forest is the realm of all those spiritual energies which surround and watch our lives. In this play Soyinka employs both the concept of the forest as the abode of secret forces always interacting with mortal life, and that of the dance as the visible expression of an interplay between one plane of reality and another. It is characteristic of African 'rites of passage' that no man can pass directly from one state of life to the next. He must formally abandon the old state before he can enter the new, and this transitional phase may be marked by a sojourn in the secret groves of the forest, just as it may be marked by a state of trance or possession, or by the elaborate death and resurrection ritual recorded by Parrinder.

Hence both the forest and the dance motifs upon which this play is based are drawn from a deep layer of African spiritual experience, whatever parallels we may find for them in Shakespeare's Forest of Arden or in the typical structure of classical comedies involving change of character or the restitution of lost power, amity or love. Shakespeare himself, after all, drew most of his comic plots from very ancient materials, instinct with the primitive myth and ritual of Greece and the Near East. The main value of his example may well have been to draw Soyinka's attention to the amount of similar material awaiting fuller dramatic exploitation in his own society.

But *A Dance of the Forests* was also the play of an occasion, the celebration of Nigerian independence. Hence Soyinka brings together in the conception of the play the idea of an important event among the living, which he calls 'The Gathering of the Tribes', and the idea of a divinely-ordered confrontation between certain mortals and their historical prototypes of a distant age.

The mortals have in fact brought this confrontation upon themselves by asking the spirits to send them certain forefathers of the glorious past to take part in their celebration. But the past which Soyinka evokes is human rather than abstractly 'glorious' and it is not a closed chapter; its bitterness and discontent have long been pressing unheeded upon the walls of the living world.

The principal divine actor in the play is Forest Father, masquerading to the mortals as a man called Obaneji; he may to some extent be identified with the god Osanyin. For the messenger and agent of Osanyin is traditionally Aroni, and it is Aroni 'the Lame One' who opens the play for us with a Prologue. He warns us that the two obscure and accusing forefathers he had selected in answer to the mortals' request have been chosen because 'In previous life they were linked in violence and blood with four of the living'. He names these four as Rola, now as then a whore by nature and hence eternally nicknamed Madame Tortoise; Demoke, now a carver and then a poet; Adenebi, now Council Orator and then Court Historian; and Agboreko, Elder of the Sealed Lips, who is a type of cryptic soothsayer in both existences, an intermediary between the living and the spirits of the forest. We learn also that the Dead Man and Woman who come in response to their appeal are a former captain and his wife from the army of the ancient emperor Mata Kharibu. Aroni now tells us that Demoke has been guilty of killing his apprentice Oremole, by plucking him down from a treetop which they were carving together in honour of the occasion. This crime completes the pattern of interaction of past and present which the Dance will reveal. But, quite apart from its ancient echoes, it has placed two of the gods in bitter enmity over Demoke. For Ogun, patron of all carvers with metal upon wood, his protegé Demoke can do no wrong. In the words of one of his praise-songs:

> The lion never allows anybody to play with his cub,
> Ogun will never allow his child to be punished.

But Demoke has chosen to carve *araba*, the silk-cotton tree sacred to Oro, god of punishment and the dead. Furthermore, Oremole, whom Demoke has killed through envy of his better head for climbing, was a devotee of Oro. Hence Oro seeks to revenge himself upon Demoke through one of his own aspects, Eshuoro, 'the wayward flesh of Oro'. Eshuoro appears in fact to be a composite of Eshu, Yoruba god of fate, mischief and the unpredictable, and Oro. Although Ogun is presented as friendly to the creative aspirations of mankind, this divine rivalry between Ogun and Eshuoro has nothing to do with Forest Father's desire to lead the four mortal principals to a deeper knowledge of themselves, and may to some extent run counter to it. It constantly threatens to disrupt the Dance, which is the focus of all Forest Father's intentions.

A glance at the structure of the play is necessary to its interpretation. Having outlined for us the situation in which the action opens, Aroni hops away and leaves us with an empty stage. Soon the surface begins to break up and the Dead Man and Woman emerge slowly from the ground. He is filthy and mouldy-looking, while she is bloated with pregnancy. Obaneji watches from a distance while they are successively rejected by Demoke, Rola and Adenebi, all of whom refuse brusquely to 'hear their case'. The dead pair wander off and Obaneji begins to lead these three mortals deeper and deeper into the forest, to become witnesses at the Dance of their former selves. They, on the other hand, believe that they are fleeing the celebrations in spontaneous disgust. Rola is appalled by the arrival of so many obscure relatives demanding hospitality for the event. Demoke is vaguely troubled by his unadmitted crime, and Adenebi claims to be overexcited by his own sense of history:

> The accumulated heritage—that is what
> we are celebrating. Mali, Chaka, Songhai.
> Glory. Empires.[1]

But, as the Dead Woman has already pointed out, the living can never order the past to their own liking, for:

> The world is big but the dead are bigger.
> We've been dying since the beginning . . .[1]

In the manner of *A Midsummer Night's Dream*, Soyinka now alternates scenes involving mortals and immortals, as Obaneji (Forest Father) leads his three chosen victims deeper and deeper into the forest, bringing them to judgement. But his method, as Agboreko points out, is 'To let the living condemn themselves'.[2] By posing as a Court Clerk, he induces Adenebi to reveal to us that he is a corrupt Councillor, responsible for licensing an overloaded lorry in which sixty-five people have been burnt to death. Rola also reveals that she is at the centre of a recent scandal in which two of her lovers died, one by murder and the other by suicide. But it is the actual sight of the dead pair, who briefly appear again, that induces Demoke finally to admit his own crime. The play, hitherto written in a fairly colloquial prose, here breaks into verse for the first time, as Demoke passionately relives the exultation of the act itself. The guilt he feels finds no expression in his words:

> I plucked him down!
> Demoke's head is no woman's cloth, spread
> To receive wood shavings from a carpenter.
> Down, down I plucked him, screaming on Oro.
> Before he made hard obeisance to his earth,
> My axe was executioner at Oro's neck. Alone,
> Alone I cut the stands that mocked me, till head
> And boastful slave lay side by side, and I
> Demoke, sat on the shoulders of the tree,
> My spirit set free and singing, my hands,
> My father's hands possessed by demons of blood . . .[3]

Obaneji and his companions are followed at a distance by another group of townsfolk, whose concern is to drive off by noise and smoke the unwholesome guests whom they unwit-

---

[1] *Ibid.*, p. 11. [2] *Ibid.*, p. 4. [3] *Ibid.*, p. 37. [4] *Ibid.*, p. 27-8.

tingly invited from the 'understreams' of death. Demoke's father, who guesses and fears his son's crime on the *araba* tree, makes one of this group. Agboreko, knowing far more than he cares to reveal, bustles to and fro between the Forest Spirits and both groups of mortals, muttering gnomic proverbs to himself. When flogger, drummers and dancers enter to clear a space for a dance, he settles down to throw palm kernels for the Ifa oracle, supposedly to find out what has happened to Rola and Demoke. But the occasion, although arranged by the living, has all the qualities of an overture for the Dance of Welcome to the dead which Obaneji is planning deeper in the forest. Even the songs of the Dirge Man carry this insistence:

> A touch, at that rounded moment of the night
> And the dead return to life,
> Dum-belly woman, plantain-breasted
> Mother! What human husband folds
> His arms and blesses randy ghosts?
> Keep away now, leave, leave the dead
> Some room to dance.[1]

The occasion is in any event shattered by the clamorous arrival of an ancient lorry named the Chimney of Ereko, summoned by the Council for its exceptional smoking and stinking properties so that it may help to drive off the forest creatures, and the unwelcome dead along with them. Adenebi, who had temporarily fled from the probings of Obaneji, is making half-hearted attempts to join this group of townsfolk, but the others panic and leave him facing the lorry alone. In mortal terror at last, he resigns himself to follow Obaneji and his little party wherever they may lead. Only the flimsiest barrier now separates him from open confession of his guilt as he hurries after them deep into the forest.

In a rapid bridge-scene we learn that Eshuoro is seeking out Demoke, intent upon revenge. But Forest Father has his own design for the regeneration of the living and does not

---

[1] *Ibid.*, pp. 40–1.

intend that either Eshuoro or Ogun shall disturb it. His preparations are now complete and he empowers Aroni, his Master of Ceremonies, to begin. While the townsfolk, far away, are intent upon their 'gathering of the tribes', the design of Forest Father for the self-discovery of the living and the dead unfolds itself. The ceremony is in three parts: first, the re-enacting of the ancient scene which prefigured the crimes of the living actors; second, the questioning of the dead pair; and last, the dance of welcome for them, which the living have refused to perform. Suddenly, like a masque, we see before us the court of the African emperor Mata Kharibu, some eight centuries ago. His queen is recognizably Madame Tortoise and the Court Poet is, equally clearly, Demoke. The queen is bored and entertains herself by sending him to catch her canary on the steep, dangerous roof of the palace. But the poet cravenly sends his pupil instead and the pupil, falling, breaks his arm. Meanwhile, the furious Emperor has summoned a Captain who has refused to serve him in an unjust and frivolous war. This warrior is the Dead Man. Their dialogue prefigures Soyinka's own encounter, seven years later, with an authority equally bent on war. When Mata Kharibu is about to strike him dead, the Physician steps forward to reason with 'the traitor':

PHYSICIAN: Was ever a man so bent on his own destruction?
WARRIOR: If that referred to the king, you have spoken your first true word today.
PHYSICAN: Future generations will label you traitor . . .
WARRIOR: Unborn generations will be cannibals, most worshipful Physician. Unborn generations will, as we have done, eat up one another . . . I took up soldiering to defend my country, but those to whom I gave the power to command my life abuse my trust in them.
PHYSICIAN: Liar! Is Mata Kharibu not your general!
WARRIOR: Mata Kharibu is leader, not merely of soldiers, but of men. Let him turn the unnatural pattern of men always eating up one another.

> I am suddenly weary of this soldiering where
> men must find new squabbles for their cruelty.[1]

The anxious courtiers consult the Historian (our old friend Adenebi) as to whether the annals show any precedent for this dangerous disease of independent thought. But the records are reassuring:

MATA KHARIBU: Did you find anything?

HISTORIAN: There is no precedent, you Highness.

MATA KHARIBU: You have looked thoroughly?

HISTORIAN: It is unheard of. War is the only consistency that past ages afford us. It is the legacy that new nations seek to perpetuate. Patriots are grateful for wars. Soldiers have never questioned bloodshed. The cause is always the accident, your Majesty, and war is the Destiny. This man is a traitor. He must be in the enemy's pay.[2]

So, despite the ominous warnings of the Soothsayer (Agboreko), Mata Kharibu plunges on with his war and the warrior is sold into slavery. But first the queen, attracted by his courage and maddened by his indifference, tries to seduce him and make him her weapon against the king. Already, we learn, she has systematically debauched his followers. The warrior, however, remains constant to his curious concept of honour. Madame Tortoise orders that he be gelded as well as enslaved, and his pregnant wife (the Dead Woman) collapses in a final agony of grief.

Now the imperial stage darkens once more and the lights return us to Forest Father. Immediately Eshuoro bursts in upon him, demanding vengeance against Demoke. He has no patience with this pantomime. But Forest Father refuses him the simple vengeance he craves, remarking, 'It is enough that they discover their own generation.' He insists that the Questioning of the Dead Pair be proceeded with. They are asked to give an account of themselves and of their coming hither.

---

[1] *Ibid.*, pp. 55–6.   [2] *Ibid.*, p. 57.

The Dead Woman insists that she is a delegate for every mother cheated by death of her fulfilment:

> Wet runnels
> Of the earth brought me hither.
> Call Forest Head, Say someone comes
> For all the rest. Say someone asks—
> Was it for this, for this,
> Children plagued their mothers?[1]

But the masked Questioner mocks the Dead Pair with such hostility that he arouses the suspicions of Aroni, who unmasks him to expose the furious countenance of Eshuoro.

Forest Father now orders that the Dance of Welcome be performed. The three mortals are masked and led into the arena. They are in a tranced state beyond themselves and have become momentarily one with the Forest. Through their masks speak the spirits of the unborn, while the Dead Man, Woman and Half-Child (now taken from his mother's womb) wait to hear whether future ages will offer that gleam of light refused by the past and the present. But the vision of the future unfolded by the Spirits of the Palm, the Darkness and the Waters, who speak respectively through Rola, Demoke, and Adenebi, is one of unremitting suffering and hopelessness:

> the shutters of the leaves
> Shall close down on the doomed
> And naked head.

The Ants also speak for all those nameless millions who will toil and die in the service of other tyrannies:

> We are the headless bodies when
> The spade of progress delves.

The Interpreter carefully orchestrates all these cries of un-remitting disaster until the exasperated Aroni intervenes, sensing that this vision of darkness has been conjured up to show the futility of any appeal for justice against fate.

---

[1] *Ibid.*, p. 69.

Meanwhile, the Half-Child pleads to be released from his endless cycle of frustrated birth, and the Dead Woman that her womb may rest at last. Their plight draws from Soyinka two of his most beautiful dramatic songs, cast like antiphons against the mounting frenzy of the Spirits:

HALF-CHILD: I who yet await a mother
                Feel this dread,
                Feel this dread,
                I who flee from womb
                To branded womb, cry it now
                I'll be born dead
                I'll be born dead . . .[1]

DEAD-WOMAN: Better not to know the bearing
                Better not to bear the weaning
                I who grow the branded navel
                Shudder at the visitation
                Shall my breast again be severed
                Again and yet again be severed
                From its right of sanctity?
                Child, your hand is pure as sorrow
                Free me of the endless burden,
                Let this gourd, let this gourd
                Break beyond my hearth . . .[2]

While a masked Interpreter calls upon the Spirits to speak in turn, a sinister Figure in Red dogs the footsteps of the Half-Child. There follows an elaborate charade described in the stage-directions to the published play, in which the Half-Child strives to touch his mother's hand but is cheated again by the Figure in Red (Eshuoro) and the Interpreter (his Jester). Just as their hands are about to meet and free him forever from 'the branded womb', three obscene and bloody Triplets enter and begin to toss the child to and fro. Demoke, who has now come to himself, dashes into the ring and snatches the child. He hands him to the Dead Woman, hoping thereby to save him from being eternally ground by the wheel of birth and death. But the final words of Forest Father, as he closes the Dance,

---

[1] Ibid., p. 74.

[2] Ibid., p. 80–1.

suggest that Demoke may at best have opened the pathway towards his own redemption. No simple action of the living can now redeem the child from the grim verdict of history:

FOREST FATHER: Yet I must do this alone, and no more, since to intervene is to be guilty of contradiction, and yet to remain altogether unfelt is to make my long-rumoured ineffectuality complete; hoping that when I have tortured awareness from their souls, that perhaps, only perhaps, in new beginnings . . . Aroni, does Demoke know the meaning of his act?

ARONI: Demoke, you hold a doomed thing in your hand.
It is no light matter to reverse the deed that was begun many lives ago. The Forest will not let you pass.[1]

Another dumb-show follows, staged perhaps in back-projection upon a drop-cloth. The villagers are seen dancing round a silhouette of Demoke's totem-pole, while Demoke himself is forced by Eshuoro to climb it with a sacrificial basket on his head representing, perhaps, the burden of his own guilt. When he climbs out of sight, Eshuoro fires the tree, but Ogun catches the falling carver and bears him on to the forestage where, chased by the growing light of dawn, he leaves him. Demoke's father enters with the beaters, who have been driving off the Forest Spirits. He finds the three chastened mortals just awaking to themselves. They speak in cryptic terms of their night of 'translation', and Demoke closes the play with a speech of exceptional impenetrability.

In the 1960 production of the play, Soyinka substituted a wooden *ibeji* (twin-figure) for the Half-Child in the tossing scene. He also simplified the final struggle between Eshuoro and Ogun by making it a straightforward duel with club and cutlass. Disturbed by the dawn, they leave the mortals to be discovered on the stage by the anxious townsfolk.

---

[1] *Ibid.*, p. 82.

The modifications which he made in production to Part Two of the play do not, however, address themselves to its real weaknesses. It will be seen that much of Part Two reads more like the synopsis of a symbolic ballet than a self-sufficient dramatic text. In his laudable desire to develop a 'total theatre' for West Africa, a theatre which will make the fullest use of music, masquerade, dance and mime, Soyinka has fallen into the error of offering us, in these final scenes, a text which is too thin and unexplicit to guide us through a complex maze of stage action performed to music alone. The relative crudity of the play-within-the-play as a device for presenting the interaction of past and present is at least clear and effective, but the devices he adopts for showing the complementary interaction of present and future are likely to fail dramatically through sheer obscurity. The various Spirits, the Ants, the Figure in Red, the Questioner, the Interpreter and the Triplets present an apparatus which is too elaborate for its purpose, which is the simple one of underlining the limited scope of Forest Father's intervention in the repetitive follies of men and gods. The back-projection scene by the totem-pole, suggested in the main printed text, is also a piece of staging whose complexity is not justified by its apparent significance; the contest between Eshuoro and Ogun has already occupied enough dramatic time and threatens to become a bore. There are also some baffling loose ends. For instance, the last speeches made by the three mortals at the end of the play give us clues linking each of them with one of the Spirits who spoke through them during the Dance of Welcome; but the Spirits of Precious Stones, of Volcanoes and of the Pachyderms, who also speak, are not accounted for.

The great pity about these difficulties is that they make it unlikely that the play will often be staged, in Africa or elsewhere. Despite its many passages of effective dramatic writing, especially in Part One, it finally emerges as more a dramatic poem than a play for the theatre. And yet it lacks the textual self-sufficiency of a good dramatic poem (such as the Auden and Isherwood *Ascent of F6*) because so much of its later action is described rather than verbally realized. Its real importance seems at first to lie in its character of an over-stored treasure house, full of themes, concepts and images of divine intervention which Soyinka was to return to and refine in much of his later writing. Yet it is possible to see the difficulties of *A Dance of the Forests* as an acting text in more positive terms and to find them almost inseparable from the poet's intentions.

In an important recent essay, *The Fourth Stage*, Soyinka has elaborated his ideas about the relationship between human and divine action. Both gods and men, he argues, are conscious of a 'primeval severance' lying between them and both constantly strive to bridge it by means of ritual. The gods to whom appeal is made in sacrifice and ceremonies of appeasement are not indifferent and aloof, but are themselves filled with the anguish of that severance and continually yearning towards reunification with men. This is the real meaning of that moment when the celebrant is possessed by his god, so central to all African religious observance, and this moment can be realized only in music, the true language of tragedy, with its concomitants of dance, mime and masquerade.

Not only are the gods filled with the anguish of severance but it was one of them, Ogun, who first launched himself into 'the gulf of transition' in a supreme effort to achieve reunification with man:

> The first actor was therefore Ogun, first suffering deity, first darer and conqueror of transition. And the first art was the tragic art . . . In tragic consciousness the votary's psyche reaches out beyond the realm of nothingness, potentially destructive of human awareness, into areas of terror and blind energies because it was the gods, the eternal presences, who first became aware of their own incompletion. Anguish is therefore primal transmission of the god's despair, vast, numinous, always incomprehensible. In vain we seek to recapture it in words, there is only the certainty of the existence of this abyss—the tragic victim plunges into it in spite of ritualistic earthing and is redeemed only by action. Without acting, and yet in spite of it, he is forever lost in the maul of tragic tyranny.

And acting is therefore a contradiction of the tragic spirit, yet it is also its natural complement. To act, the Promethean instinct of rebellion, channels anguish into creative purpose which releases man from a totally destructive despair, releasing from within him the most energic, deeply combative inventions which, without usurping the territory of the infernal gulf, bridge them with visionary hopes ... At the charged climactic moments of the tragic rites we understand how music came to *contain*, the sole art form which does contain, tragic reality.[1]

Looking again at the play in the light of these ideas, we see how precisely Demoke's nature echoes, on a human level, all the divine attributes of his mentor Ogun. For there is a demonic and destructive element in the nature of 'the darer' (we may think of Milton's Satan also launching himself courageously into the gulf of transition, but for the *ruin* of mankind), and Demoke has to suffer both the experience of that violence within him and the knowledge that it is there. When Demoke leaps to save the Half-Child he is attempting a tragic action in the void that separates one area of existence from another. As an artist he shares the ambivalent creative energy of Ogun, an energy which *changes* the world and which must inevitably bear the seeds of violence within it. Again, when Demoke attempts to climb the *araba* tree with a sacrificial basket on his head, he is daring the perils of disintegration which assail all those who venture into the gulf of transition. His fall from the burning tree and his snatching-up by Ogun may be seen as a symbolic enactment of death and rebirth or of disintegration and recreation. And the absence of expository dialogue at these crucial instants of the tragic action may be seen as consistent with Soyinka's belief that these are precisely the points at which the action must pass from words into music.

It is the very profundity of the play's meaning which makes me a little sceptical of interpretations which would see the

---

[1] 'The Fourth Stage'; in *The Morality of Art*, ed. Jefferson (Routledge and Kegan Paul, 1969), pp. 123-4.

Half-Child simply as representing the destiny of Nigeria, now to be saved at Independence by a change in the hearts of men of which Demoke's action is symbolic. My feeling is rather that Soyinka does not believe in collective salvations at all: it lies in the breast of every man to find his particular god and strive continually towards unity with him. The harmony for which Forest Father strives is both vertical and lateral. On the vertical plane, man and god yearn towards one another: on the lateral plane, the several aspects of a once united godhead also yearn to be gathered up once more. The play is thus addressed to the regeneration of man rather than to any temporal political concept which ignores man's immemorial nature.

In the years since *A Dance of the Forests*, Soyinka's gift for satire has been employed mainly, as in his novel *The Interpreters* and his play *The Road*, at the service of his essentially tragic vision of life. His belief that civilisation has been purchased only with terrible difficulty and at terrible cost, that it remains continually in peril from the philistinism and tyrannical appetites of men in power, informs almost everything he writes. Expressions of purely satirical intent have been confined to a few short poems and to the sketches in his three stage reviews.

From 1960 to 1963 Soyinka continued to be based mainly in Ibadan and to make that city the centre of his theatrical activities. During 1961 he helped to found the Mbari Writers and Artists Club, whose first premises were an ex night-club in the very centre of the city. In the small open-air theatre which, together with an art gallery and restaurant, composed its premises, he directed another production of *Brother Jero* during September 1961, in which the part of the Prophet Jeroboam was played by Yemi Lijadu and that of his assistant Chume by Ralph Okpara. Both of these leading actors were now working for Radio Nigeria in Lagos, so that the continual travelling between the two cities remained a feature of every production by the 1960 Masks. Another of these took place during the middle months of 1961, the first performance of *Dear Parent and Ogre*, a mildly political comedy by the Sierra

Leone author Sarif Easmon. In this production, which was presented at the Arts Theatre, Ibadan, Soyinka doubled as director and leading man, in the part of the politician Dauda Touray, whilst Segun Olusola, another actor now much associated with his work, appeared as the young trade union leader Mahmoud Sawaneh. This rather mannered and conventional comedy became acceptable entertainment in a well-conceived and skilful production, and Soyinka's performance in the part of the elderly, somewhat pompous, but still dominating Prime Minister, added greatly to his reputation as an actor.

In the following year he was again able to present the first work of a fellow African dramatist, when he directed the 1960 Masks production of *Song of a Goat*, a full-length verse tragedy by the young Nigerian poet John Pepper Clark. In this production, which took place on the open-air stage at the Mbari Club, a live goat was sacrificed during the central scene of the action. This controversial and deliberate gesture probably contributed to the appearance of a similar scene in *The Interpreters* a couple of years later. The first performance of this difficult, perilously-poised play foundered in the laughter with which African audiences so often greet any tragedy with which they cannot immediately relate their own experience, if they have even the slightest encouragement from words or actors. The second performance was, however, in the opinion of many who saw it, the best this play has ever enjoyed.

In the meantime Soyinka had written two more plays, the radio piece *Camwood on the Leaves* and the short tragedy *The Strong Breed*. The former was performed on Radio Nigeria with Francesca Pereira in the leading female role. It has never been published and it must be assumed that Soyinka does not regard it as part of the permanent canon of his plays. Some of the ideas in it have been more effectively developed in his other works. *The Strong Breed*, a work of considerable beauty and, in its later scenes, concentration of effect, had to wait a long time for its first stage performance. It is the only one of his plays to have been published before performance, for it appeared along with *The Swamp Dwellers* and *The Trails of Brother Jero* in a well-designed Mbari Club publication of 1963, entitled *Three Plays*. In the same year, the Oxford University Press published *The Lion and the Jewel* and *A Dance of the Forests* as separate volumes, thereby bringing to five the number of his works available to a public increasingly hungry for African plays for performance in schools, clubs and theatres.

Soyinka himself transcribed a part of *The Strong Breed* for an Esso International film about Nigeria called *Culture in Transition* and the play was also produced on Nigerian television, but the first full stage production was mounted during 1966, directed by Derek Bullock and Miss Chris Groves with students of Government College, Ibadan, and St Anne's Girls School, Ibadan. This much praised production was soon followed by one directed by the outstanding Nigerian actress Betty Okotie, which was presented at the World Festival of University Drama at Nancy in April 1967 and at the Arts Theatre, Ibadan, in the following month. This production was awarded the Third Prize at the Festival. It is difficult to account for this relatively long delay in testing *The Strong Breed* in stage conditions for, although it makes some demands upon the ingenuity of the director and designer, these appear to be challenging rather than insuperable. In the following chapter we shall examine this play as an important stage in the unfolding of Soyinka's tragic vision of the artist as sacrifice; the one who, matching the daring of his patron god Ogun, plunges into the gulf of transition in a supreme effort to reach new areas of awareness. By placing it in the context of his other tragedies, we shall see its importance as a link between the first expression of his ideas in *A Dance of the Forests* and their mature fulfilment in *The Road*.

3

The Tragedies

All Soyinka's tragic plots centre upon a death, and attempt through their action to evaluate that death for those who survive. Thus Soyinka restores to the word 'tragic' its proper weight of meaning—for the tragic death is not that which is casual, incidental or out of season, but that which is invested with significance for the community who witness it. Of the three deaths we are here concerned with, only Professor's in *The Road* can be expected to leave this community with some sense of fulfilment, of that *catharsis* which Aristotle isolated as the supreme emotional product of tragedy. For although the immediate circumstances of Professor's death may come as a surprise, the event itself has been long prepared for in his own mind and in those of his followers. Eman's sacrifice of himself in *The Strong Breed* appears to fulfil some personal destiny of his own rather than the purgative function hoped for by the town's chiefs. And although the death of Segi's father in *Kongi's Harvest* produces a cataclysm in the state, it is not quite the cataclysm he hoped for; the play ends on a question-mark. In all three plays, however, as in much of Soyinka's poetry and throughout his novel *The Interpreters*, we are conscious of the urgency of his own search for the meaning of particular deaths. For if death has no meaning, then life can have none either. If death can be made into a total gesture of being, then a man's end can sometimes have a dignity that was never apparent in his life.

(i) The Strong Breed

This is the only one of Soyinka's plays which deals specifically

46

with the theme of the scapegoat. Here again, no assiduous reading of *The Golden Bough* is necessary for an African writer seeking to lay bare the ritual springs of tragedy. Animal scapegoats were still a regular feature of Yoruba towns in the years of Soyinka's childhood, and even human ones were commonly found well into the present century. Nowadays the activities of press and politics often select targets which fulfil the same function, on both the local and the national scale. Apparently such devices are considered more civilized than the somewhat crude and forthright methods of the past; but the basis of selection is often the same.

The play opens in an atmosphere full of tension and foreboding, conveyed by Soyinka with some economy and skill. It is the eve of the new year and all the town is preparing for the festival. But Eman, a stranger to the town who has come here to work as a dispenser, is being hurried away from the scene by his distraught sweetheart Sunma. Eman has befriended a crippled boy called Ifada, but Sunma suddenly rounds upon the boy and drives him away. Eman remarks in astonishment:

> It is almost as if you are forcing
> yourself to hate him, Why?

Sunma remains evasive, but gradually Eman realises that the townspeople have picked on Ifada for their annual scapegoat and that Sunma is trying to get her lover away on the pretext of a change of air so that he will not see the evil that is being done or endanger himself by involvement in it. Indeed, Sunma herself seems almost frantic with a sense of this evil lurking in her own family and clan. While Eman and Sunma quarrel over her demand that they leave the town for a day or two, a sinister pantomime is enacted just outside their hut. A strange Girl enters pulling a cloth 'carrier' by a string. Seeing Ifada, she contemptuously asks him to beat the carrier for her so that it may bear away her sickness. Later they will perhaps tie it to a tree and burn it. They exit, with Ifada joyously beating out a prelude to the fate that is already hanging over himself.

Meanwhile the lorry that might have carried Eman and

Sunma away has been heard in the distance sounding its last call for passengers and moving off. They are trapped, but as yet Sunma seems to feel this far more strongly than Eman. For all that she is a native of the town, her destiny insists that she leave it, whereas Eman's equally obscurely insists upon his remaining to meet whatever may befall. Sunma sees that she is completely shut out from his real preoccupations; it is as if he were continually expiating something in his past which excludes her. A darkness falls outside the hut, they discuss their plight with a kind of flat despair which is reflected, unfortunately, in the stilted quality of certain speeches:

SUNMA: Now the thought will not leave me, I have a feeling which will not be shaken off, that in some way, you have tonight totally destroyed my life.

EMAN: You are depressed, you don't know what you are saying.

SUNMA: Don't think I am accusing you. I say all this only because I cannot help it.

EMAN: We must not remain shut up here. Let us go and be part of the living.

SUNMA: No, Leave them alone.[1]

Soyinka is over-intent upon charging these brief exchanges with 'significance'. The result is that they fail to live as dramatic dialogue and give the actors a difficult time hereabouts. This scene would benefit from cutting and tightening up in performance. Meanwhile, in the gloom outside, we have seen the Girl return, closely followed by Ifada, who is suddenly seized and bundled away by two men. The Girl runs off, leaving her 'carrier' at Eman's doorstep. When he goes to pick it up, Sunma makes a last attempt to ward off a fate which seems inexorably to involve him. But the sight of the carrier is followed by that of Ifada himself, who enters desperate with fear and seeking refuge with the one friend he knows. Sunma is now swept aside by everyone; Eman insists upon harbouring Ifada,

---

[1] *Ibid.*, pp. 247–8.

Alu (Christine Clinton) and Makuri (Adisa Ajetunmodi) in the Ibadan Arts Theatre production of The Swamp Dwellers, *1959.*

Elizabeth Osisioma as Sidi in the Orisun Players' 1964 production of The Lion and the Jewel, *directed by Wole Soyinka.*

Aroni and Forest Father (Wole Soyinka) in the 1960 Masks production of A Dance of the Forests.

(Overleaf) *Samson (Bari Johnson) and Murano (Dapo Adelugba) in the 1965 London production of* The Road.

while her father Jaguna, arriving in pursuit of the lost scapegoat, insists upon her being carried home and locked up for the night. When Eman taunts Jaguna and his fellow chiefs for using an unwilling and terrified idiot for their carrier, Jaguna taunts him in return:

> JAGUNA: You say there are no men in this village because they cannot provide a willing carrier. And yet I heard Oroge tell you we only use strangers. There is only one other stranger in this village, but I have not heard him offer himself. It is so easy to talk is it not?[1]

Everything in the play hitherto has been conspiring to put Eman in Ifada's place and the audience has been fully prepared for this development. Soyinka now breaks up his action into a series of brief unlocalized scenes moving towards the climax of Eman's death. The first of these, however, is a rather superfluous and unsuccessful demonstration that Eman has in fact taken over the carrier's role. After a short black-out Ifada is seen to reappear, now free of fear, and begin stripping the toy carrier of its clothes. The Girl disturbs him and they fight, but the struggle is broken up by the return of Sunma. Seeing Ifada there, she realizes what has happened and drags him off to help her find Eman, overwhelming him with threats and menaces. No explanation is offered for Sunma's reappearance (Jaguna has just given strict instructions for her to be locked up overnight), and this, coupled with the generally contrived nature of the scene, makes it one of the weaker points of the play's construction.

Next we see Eman hiding between two huts (by the use of selective lighting, the same stage-set can be used throughout and the play acted without a break); he is now dressed as a carrier and has broken away from his pursuers. Two of these, Jaguna and the more reflective Oroge, enter in pursuit and we learn from their conversation that Eman fled from them after the very first stage of his punishment. Jaguna puts this down

---

[1] *Ibid.*, p. 255.

to simple cowardice, but Oroge believes that something else, some desire for ultimate rejection, is driving him onward. Immediately we see Eman again, now thirsty, bleeding and exhausted, gazing transfixed at a vision of his dead father. The old man is preparing to carry the sins of his town for the last time and we learn that Eman has refused to take over the hereditary role which should by right have passed to him. As his father gets ready to carry the dwarf boat which represents the sins and suffering of the whole community a younger, bitterer Eman enters (it can be the same actor, for the contemporary Eman is now in darkness). The father speaks:

OLD MAN: Come nearer . . . we will never meet again, son. Not on this side of the flesh. What I do not know is whether you will return to take my place.

EMAN: I will never come back.

OLD MAN: Do you know what you are saying? Ours is a strong breed my son. It is only a strong breed that can take this boat to the river year after year and wax stronger on it. I have taken down each year's evils for over twenty years. I hoped you would follow me.

EMAN: My life here died with Omae.

OLD MAN: Omae died giving birth to your child and you think the world is ended. Eman, my pain did not begin when Omae died. Since you sent her to stay with me son, I lived with the burden of knowing that this child would die bearing your son.

EMAN: Father . . .

OLD MAN: Don't you know that it was the same with you? And me? No woman survives the bearing of the strong ones. Son, it is not the mouth of the boaster that says he belongs to the strong breed. It is the tongue that is red with pain and black with sorrow. Twelve years you were away my son, and for those twelve years I knew the love of an old man for his daughter and the pain of a man helplessly awaiting his loss.[1]

---

[1] *Ibid.*, pp. 259–60.

So now we understand the whole complex of past desertions from which Eman is still running; desertion of his sweetheart Omae, desertion of his father and desertion of his role. In another 'flash-back' scene soon after we see Eman disturbed in the circumcision hut by the young Omae. He is now a boy of fourteen, but already he treats her with the same obscure ruthlessness which was to exclude Sunma from his life many years later. He deserts both the hut and his lecherous tutor (here we get the same rejection of the more restrictive aspects of tradition as in *The Swamp Dwellers*), but it is not to go with Omae. Instead, he despatches her to live with his father and to await his return from a journey whose motives are as dark to himself as to all those who love him. It is as though the current of energy which should make him a carrier has somehow gone astray, driving him to an unfruitful destruction and flight.

Meanwhile Jaguna and Oroge, whose pursuit punctuates these visions of Eman's past, have decided that he will now have to die in order to purge the extra contamination brought by his flight from punishment and lack of preparation. Normally it would be enough to flog him through the village and out into the bush, never to return. But, playing upon his need of water, they guard all the wells and set a death-trap upon the only path leading to the river. In all this they are assisted by the young Girl, who tricks Eman and tries to get him captured. She is the play's most sinister character, since she seems to represent corrupted innocence and a mute indifference to sorrow and suffering.

Events now move swiftly to a climax. After a last glimpse of Eman and his father, rigid with grief at the graveside of Omae, we suddenly see them again on the pathway to the stream. The father is now carrying the boat and, fearing his son's death, tries to direct him by another path. But Eman is now irresistibly drawn to embrace his father's fate. He follows the running figure and we hear the hideous twang as he springs the trap and is hung dangling in the branches of the sapling. His death has been compassed at last, but it brings no comfort or relief to anyone. Jaguna's

nis daughter has been poisoned into hate and
ous violence as he beats down her protests. In the
/s final words, he and Oroge complain that the
villagers have gazed on the hanging body with fear and
guilt rather than rejoicing:

> JAGUNA: Women could not have behaved so shamefully.
> One by one they crept off like sick dogs. Not one
> could raise a curse.
>
> OROGE: It was not only him they fled. Do you see how
> unattended we are?[1]

They go miserably off, leaving upon the stage a tableau which
unites the play's only hint of love and reconciliation with its
abiding quality of horror; as Ifada cradles and comforts the
broken Sunma, the Girl stands in the bushes impassively
watching them. Her little carrier, which she has hung from a
tree nearby, has been no more effective than the human one,
it seems, in purging an immemorial sickness.

Eman's death fails of its sacramental intention for the
community as a whole, though it may help to regenerate love
between Sunma and Ifada, the only survivors who are not
tainted with collective guilt. Soyinka implies that the tradition of the willing carrier which is Eman's inheritance is one
worthy of respect, in that it dignifies both the suffering of the
hero and the witness of the spectators. His rejection of such
characters as the gross Kadiye and the hateful Jaguna does not,
as some critics have supposed, amount to a rejection of
traditional religious ideas. On the contrary, it is the best of these
ideas, together with the ritual and mythology which embody
them, that have provided his richest store of metaphor and
dramatic symbol; but they call out for reinterpretation in
terms of ever-changing values and conditions. A man like
Eman's father, who understands the nature of his task and
never swerves from its fulfilment, is a worthy bearer of the
tragic role. And in *The Road*, the finest of Soyinka's published
plays, such a character appears to stand at the very centre of
the tragic action.

(ii) The Road (1965)

The Professor, hero of *The Road*, is a man wholly dedicated to the knowledge of death, which he has rightly understood as the sole access to the meaning of life itself. By living in the presence of death he seeks to complete this knowledge and to prepare his followers, to the limit of their capacities, for their own fatal vocation as men of the road. The benefit which Professor's death confers upon the living is directly related to his role as a sort of teacher, guide or forerunner. Explaining the nature of his own search, he says:

> The Word may be found companion not to
> life, but death.[1]

Now the Word which Professor seeks is surely the all-creating Word which expresses the indestructible energy of God. Although he seeks this Word in the presence and process of death, his concern is thus seen as a vital, not a morbid one. His is also learning to master the fear of death which often inhibits the fullness of life. 'One must cheat fear,' he says, 'by foreknowledge.'[2]

All the characters in the play stand at some measurable distance from the full knowledge of death that Professor is seeking, and he judges them accordingly. Closest to the reality of death when the play opens is Murano, Professor's mysterious deaf-and-dumb wine-tapper who appears only at twilight and vanishes at dawn. Murano is in what Yorubas call the *agemo* phase. Newly dead, he is still in the phase of physical dissolution and gradual withdrawal from the visible world.

Evidence that this *agemo* concept is not uniquely African may be found in a remarkable passage in D. H. Lawrence's great novel *Women in Love*, where Rupert Birkin and Gerald Crich are discussing the nature of death and dissolution:

> 'There's a long way to go, after the point of intrinsic death, before we disappear,' said Birkin.
>
> 'There is,' said Gerald. 'But what sort of way?' He seemed

---

[1] *Ibid.*, p. 275.   [2] *The Road* (O.U.P., 1965), p. 11.   [3] *Ibid.*, p. 94.

to press the other man for knowledge which he himself knew far better than Birkin did.

'Right down the slope of degeneration—mystic, universal degeneration. There are many stages of pure degradation to go through: age-long. We live on long after our death, and progressively, in progressive devolution.[1]

Now Murano has been killed just before the play opens, knocked down by the lorry-driver Kotonu just at the moment when he is masquerading as the god Ogun at the annual Drivers' Festival. As the play teaches us, Kotonu and his 'mate' Samson have hidden the body in the back of their lorry to deceive the angry worshippers and have brought it back to town. But Professor, finding it, has taken Murano as his companion in order that he may learn from him the ultimate secrets of physical dissolution and the return to the primal energy which underlies all existence. Explaining why Murano (like Aroni in *A Dance of the Forests*) always walks with a limp, Professor declares:

When a man has one leg in each world, his legs are never the same. The big toe of Murano's foot—the left one of course—rests on the slumbering chrysalis of the Word. When that crust cracks my friends—you and I, that is the moment we await. That is the moment of our rehabilitation.[2]

Among the group of drivers and lorry-park layabouts whose lives are dominated by Professor, the driver Kotonu is his aptest pupil. Having come closer to death than ever before, both in killing Murano and in witnessing a terrible accident at a broken bridge, Kotonu has resolved to trade in death like Professor rather than continue to gamble with it as a driver. He consents to take over the 'Aksident Store' which Professor stocks up by the systematic looting of wrecks and road-victims. For, on the level of sardonic comedy which runs right through the play, Professor's metaphysical quest for the Word expresses itself in this activity. He is also a notable forger of licences and is not above assisting the flow of accidents by

---

[1] *Women in Love*, Penguin edition, 1960, p. 229. [2] *Ibid.*, p. 45.

removing vital traffic-signs. Kotonu dimly understands the real nature of Murano, for he demands of Professor towards the end of the play whether Murano 'is the god apparent'. And there is a double irony in this question, for Murano is not only the partial presence of a newly-killed man, but that of a man killed at the very moment of his possession by Ogun, when he had literally become the god apparent. Professor replies in terms of the evening 'communion service' which they hold every day in sharing out the palm-wine brought by Murano:

> . . . it came to the same thing, that I held a god captive, that his hands held out the day's communion![1]

Kotonu's mate Samson is the play's flamboyant blurter. He has occasional flashes of insight but is quite unable to integrate them into a consistent vision of experience. Thus he keeps urging Kotonu to take the road again as a driver, but he glimpses something of Kotonu's new trade when he keeps comparing him to a spider who now waits for the flies to fall into his net. On a literal level, however, he does not realize that Kotonu is now running the despised Aksident Store. He also blames Kotonu for the accident with the masquerader; this only happened because the driver had for too long refused to run down an occasional dog and so keep Ogun satisfied. In the end, the god had demanded 'heavier meat', for his sacrifice.

Those who lie furthest from any real consciousness of death are the sinister mob of layabouts and their leader, Say Tokyo Kid. Samson is at least dedicated to the life of the road and the rituals it demands, but these are ready to turn their hands to any act of political violence or assassination for the sake of a few shillings. They are the casual agents of death, like the motor-cyclists in Cocteau's film *Orphée*, because they have no sense of the value of life. But for dramatic purposes they can also act as an undifferentiated 'chorus', who help to make possible the play's free movement in time. It is in its handling

---

[1] *Ibid.*, p. 90.

of time and space within a single scene and using a single group of actors that *The Road* displays its greatest originality. In *A Dance of the Forests* Soyinka had fallen back on the well-tried device of the-play-within-the-play to express his vision of the interaction of past and present. In *The Strong Breed* we have the periodic 'flashbacks' or visions of past life that Eman sees during his flight, though these come close to an actual coincidence with living reality in the final scene, where Eman follows his dead father towards the river. In *The Road*, however, Soyinka devises a machinery of almost frightening flexibility and economy to evoke past action; the actors literally slide into the past despite themselves when they initiate or over-intensely recall its events. To put it in another way, the 'normal' sequence of time is marked by certain climacteric instants which simultaneously include all those past or future instants which correspond with them. Just as the African masquerader communicates with the eternal in the moment of his possession by the god or spirit he is dancing for, so the imitation of any past or future action can charge the present with all its unpredictable and terrible energy. The arrival of such a moment in the play's action is often signalled by the way in which the chorus of layabouts reacts to it.

The audience is gently broken in to this idea by the early scene where Samson, caught sitting in Professor's chair and imitating him, confuses everyone's identity by imposing himself upon Professor as a visiting millionaire. Apart from its powerful echo of a similar scene in *Henry IV* Part I, where Falstaff imitates the King, this scene also serves to remind the audience how thin are the walls enclosing our sense of who we are. A little later comes the scene where Samson imitates the Professor in his former churchgoing days, when he used to insist on bowing at every mention of Jesus Christ and delicately wiping his brow with a succession of clean handkerchiefs. From the church window which dominates the back wall of the stage comes a burst of organ music, seemingly unrelated to Samson's activities, but serving to punctuate exactly the rhythm of the original scene as he plays it out. Here the organ actually performs the type of role later assumed by the chorus.

Soon after this the layabouts start dirging:

> It's a long long road to heaven[1]

while Samson is muttering to himself over Kotonu's refusal to drive any more after the fatal accident with the masquerader. Again, they dirge softly in the background when Samson and Kotonu are re-enacting the death of Kotonu's truck-pushing father, crushed against his own load of stockfish by a runaway lorry. On both occasions, this dirging underlines the mobility of the chorus's function and their ability to change the character of a scene by suddenly charging it with the energy of the past.

A simple confusion of one moment of time with another also occurs when the funeral service for the passengers killed in the accident at the bridge is held in the church behind the stage, and its organ music is mistaken by Murano for that of even-song, which usually summons him from the forest to serve the 'communion' of palm-wine to Professor and his followers. Consequently he arrives in daylight and must be hidden by Professor from their profane eyes. The layabouts have just had their heads broken by fighting at a political rally and have incurred Professor's most bitter rage:

> I offer you a purpose but you take unmeaning risks which means
> I, I must wait and hope that you return alive to fulfil the course
> I have drawn for you.[2]

A death met in such a cause would lack all dedication or significance, and so all prospect of redemption. The evening communion is intended to bring them gradually to a state of understanding and readiness, for their very trade requires them to live in the constant presence and expectation of death.

Part Two of the play opens with a re-enactment of the accident which Kotonu and Samson have witnessed. A crowded lorry had over-taken them just before the bridge and had thus been the first to go crashing through its rotten timbers,

---

[1] *Ibid.*, p. 19   [2] *Ibid.*, p. 51.

whilst Kotonu's lorry, with a screeching of brakes which is now actually heard in the theatre, managed to pull up on the brink of the chasm, here represented by the front edge of the stage. Professor insists that this disaster was also a sacrifice, demanded by the goddess of the river whose waters were running dry:

> Below that bridge, a black rise of buttocks, two unyielding thighs and that red trickle like a woman washing her monthly pain in a thin river. So many lives rush in and out between her legs, and most of it a waste.[1]

So the rhythm mounts, accustoming the audience to look for sacramental meaning in the recent events to which the play is continually reverting. Now comes the most powerful re-enactment of all. Kotonu is rummaging in the back of the lorry, upstage, which now serves as his store. Suddenly the tailboard falls with a crash and out tumbles the mask worn by the dead masquerader (Murano) at the time of the accident, closely followed by Kotonu himself. Instantly the stage is flooded with excited whip-cracking dancers and we are carried back to the terrifying moment of the accident itself. The drivers are seeking everwhere for their lost god, whom Kotonu has just knocked down and killed, hurriedly hiding the body in the back of his lorry. In order to deceive them, Kotonu must don the mask himself. But it is still full of the dead man's blood, which blinds and maddens him. His frenzied attempts to tear it off take on the appearance of a dance of possession by the god Ogun. The exhausted Kotonu falls to the ground and the triumphant dancers, still flogging each other, run off. Their exit instantly returns the stage to the present moment in which Kotonu and the mask have just tumbled from the back of the lorry.

It is now Samson's turn to undergo the experience of possession by the dead. The venal policeman Particulars Joe is still hunting for the killers of the masquerader. Searching in the lorry,

---

[1] *Ibid.*, p. 58.

he is just about to find the tell-tale mask when someone switches it with the uniform of Sergeant Burma, former manager of the Aksident Store, who has recently been killed in yet another motor accident. Samson puts on the uniform and begins to imitate the squeaky voice and big manner of Sergeant Burma to distract the policeman, but as the talk moves to the manner of Burma's death the drivers begin to sing his funeral dirge. Samson repeats the frenzied movements of Kotonu as he tears off the uniform, feeling himself suddenly identified with a dead man and with his fate.

These various patterns of imitation and possession, together with the innate power of the mask and the multiple roles of the chorus, all converge in the intensity of the play's final scene. It is now evening. Murano appears upon his proper cue and Professor can again begin his daily ritual of preparing his followers for the reality of death. The pagan communion is performed under the walls of the church, within which Professor once sought the Word in vain. Only when those walls collapse will the Word perhaps be found amongst the ruins. While he is in the midst of pouring wine for the celebrants, Murano's eye falls upon the mask still lying abandoned on the stage. Dim memories of his former life begin to stir in him and Professor, intent that everyone present shall learn to confront the fear of death, insists that he put on the mask, while he forces the drivers to play the special rhythm for the *agemo* cult:

> Do you cringe, because you are confronted by the final gate to the Word?...Do I feed you wine for nothing? Play you foul-mouthed vermin of the road![1]

Murano begins to dance and everyone becomes transfixed with dread, realizing that death itself has suddenly become apparent in their midst and none knows where it will strike. Only Professor is fully ready to meet it. In the course of a scuffle over a knife he is stabbed, apparently by accident, and falls

---

[1] *Ibid*., p. 93.

dying upon the stage. Determined to teach by the words as well as the manner of his death, Professor rouses himself for a final sermon. For the 'Knowledge' which Professor has all along been seeking is the *Ashe*, 'the Power of the Word' of Yoruba belief. Through union with his god at this crisis, Professor believes he has become an *Alashe*, a vehicle for the Word itself. So he must speak what is in him before he dies. Kotonu had insisted that the passengers in the ill-fated lorry which overtook them just before the bridge had no faces; they were already transfigured by the imminence of death. Professor reverts to this image in his final words, for the drivers must learn to cultivate a wise passiveness in the company of the doomed. Yet there is an element of sacrilege about Professor's whole proceeding, for he seeks to manipulate others (including Murano) for the sake of his own enlightenment; to penetrate *vicariously* the mystery of death. It is this sacriligious element, detected by Say Tokyo Kid in the final scene, which defeats Professor and ultimately destroys him:

> Be even like the road itself. Flatten your bellies with the hunger of an unpropitious day, power your hands with the knowledge of death . . . Dip in the same basin as the man who makes his last journey and stir with one finger, wobbling reflections of two hands, two hands, but one face only . . . [1]

While he is speaking the mask spins to a stop and falls empty upon the stage, its purpose fulfilled.

The Road marks a new level of achievement in several ways. Not only does Soyinka here discover the dramatic means for presenting his vision with swift economy and concentrated effect, but his language undergoes a comparable development. He now abandons the rather loose blank verse, occasionally over-rich in its effects, which was favoured in *A Dance of the Forests* and *The Lion and the Jewel*, though *The Road* enjoys

---

[1] *Ibid.*, p. 96.

the poetic qualities of intensity and suggestion more than any earlier play. Here the complexities are transferred to the situation underlying the words, leaving a verbal surface of salty, sharp and swiftly-moving prose. Although the content of Professor's speeches is unashamedly metaphysical, his words are sometimes startling in their brutality and directness. Kotonu and Samson range from pidgin English and fragments of Yoruba to a speech almost as formal as Professor's, the choice of language depending entirely upon the nature of the scene they are playing. When Kotonu, for example, is reflecting upon his new-found passivity, he remarks with formal simplicity:

Much more peaceful to trade in death than to witness it.[1]

Say Tokyo Kid and his gang speak throughout in the Americanized, cinema-influenced slang of the lorryparks, whilst Particulars Joe sticks closely to his stilted policeman's English. The songs themselves are all in Yoruba, hence inviting the composer to give them authentic settings, but Soyinka does offer translations for the benefit of the non-Yoruba producer. This complexity of linguistic texture is an important source of the play's strength and points the way towards a much greater use of different types and levels of language in African drama.

It is possible that the liberation of language in Soyinka's recent plays has been partly stimulated by the example of Nigeria's popular professional theatre troupes, whose influence and prestige have greatly increased over the past decade. Popular theatre parties began to flourish in Western Nigeria in the late 'forties and early 'fifties, the pioneer group being Hubert Ogunde's Theatre Party, founded in 1945. But for a long time these groups were regarded with tolerant amusement by the educated class and were not seen to be the important innovation that they were. It was the theatre parties which helped to create an urban audience for itinerant performers and which established that it was at least possible to make a

---

[1] *Ibid.*, p. 84.

moderate living for the professional player. With the introduction of traditional music and instruments by Kola Ogunmola's group in the late 'fifties, followed by that of vernacular (Yoruba) texts and traditional themes by Duro Ladipo in the early 'sixties, the existence of a distinctive new art form began to be recognized. These 'ballad operas' or 'folk operas' in which much of the text was sung and most of the rest improvised, realized the ideal of 'total theatre' towards which Soyinka's more literary work, perhaps initially influenced by Brecht, had also been tending. They united the word, sung or spoken, with dance, mime, music and gesture on a basis of absolute equality. Also they brought the drummer and the singer right on to the stage in a manner more extreme even than that of Japanese drama, since they actually mingled with and took part in the action, instead of merely commenting upon it, dictating its rhythm and lending it a voice, in the manner of the Japanese Kabuki or Nō. Recently experiments have been made by these companies with relatively stabilized and printed texts, both in Yoruba and in pidgin English, which have shown the possibilities of this form for literature as well as for popular performance. *The Road*, with its Yoruba choruses and completely integrated action, is not only a logical development from Soyinka's previous work but may also mark the beginning of a creative interplay between the burgeoning popular theatre and the more university-based drama of Ibadan and Lagos.

(iii) Kongi's Harvest (1967)

Soyinka's last published play before his prolonged imprisonment was his closest to a direct comment upon the contemporary political scene in Africa. At one level, this play is a satirical comedy upon the emergent style and rhetoric of African dictatorship. The tone of the opening songs, however, together with the brutal climax of the action, combine to give it a more sombre and disturbing quality. We do not usually associate deaths offstage and severed heads in calabashes with comic finales and it is for this reason that I have placed it more in the tradition of Soyinka's tragic writing.

66

The play's two protagonists, the old king Oba Danlola and the megalomaniac dictator Kongi, are both left in some disarray at the end of the play. Hence the farewell to past greatness and formal splendour which is sung to Danlola by his faithful courtiers in 'Hemlock', the opening movement of the play, is a farewell occasioned not only by Kongi's campaign against the king but also by Africa's search for a future which equally excludes both types of discredited leadership.

The play opens with Oba Danlola in prison, together with certain of his chiefs and followers. He is condemned to remain there until he agrees that the honour of eating the first of the New Yam, traditionally belonging to the king, must now be transferred to the new-style political boss. During this scene the brash Prison Superintendent is so outsmarted by Danlola that he is forced to abase himself to the king again and again while the royal drums break forth into a song of mourning and farewell. For the words of the song demonstrate that, however proud his spirit, the mere fact that their master is in prison is enough to convince them that the old days can never truly return again:

DANLOLA: This dance is the last
            Our feet shall dance together
            The royal python may be good
            At hissing, but it seems
            The scorpion's tail is fire.

DRUMMER: The king's umbrella
            Gives us no more shade
            But we summon no dirge-master.
            The tunnel passes through
            The hill's belly
            But we cry no defilement
            A new-dug path may lead
            To the secret heart of being.
            Ogun is still a god
            Even without his navel.[1]

---

[1] *Kongi's Harvest* (Oxford University Press, 1967), p. 9.

Although these lines express a confidence that the divine power of the gods cannot be annulled by presidential decree, yet the tone of the whole song from which they are quoted, with its reiterated refrain 'This is the last/That we shall dance together', is one of dignified withdrawal into the shades of history. As such, it prepares us for Oba Danlola's decision soon afterwards to go to the New Yam Festival and surrender his functions to Kongi, in return for the reprieve of five conspirators sentenced to death for a bomb-plot against the dictator.

The central section of the play, an alternation of rapid scenes in Kongi's mountain retreat and in an urban night-club, centres around the rather inept machinations of the Organizing Secretary. This character exhibits all the slightly menacing and false *bonhomie* of the political toadie. Prolific in threats and bribes, he represents the system of intimidation, corruption and sycophancy on which Kongi's power now rests. Carefully insulated from reality by his professional flatterers, the Leader lives more and more in a cloud-cuckoo land of self-worship and magical sloganizing. Some of the satire hereabouts is deft and some of it crude, depending for its effect upon the topicality of certain dictatorial mannerisms and pronouncements of Presidents Nkrumah and Banda. The basic follies and greeds exposed by the satire are, however, always with us, and a production of the play ten years hence would have little difficulty in finding the right lines and gestures to strike a contemporary chord.

These scenes also show us that the real opposition to Kongi does not come from Danlola and his brother-king Sarumi, but from the younger group represented by Sarumi's son Daodu and Daodu's mistress Segi. Daodu has started an infuriatingly successful co-operative farm in competition with the somewhat militaristic State Farms of the regime, while Segi, whose father is one of the condemned men, has organized her night-club as a centre of resistance employing sex and beer as two of its weapons against the pomposities of power. Segi, we gather, has even tried her methods successfully upon Kongi in the past. And it is Daodu who persuades Danlola to swallow his pride, so permitting Kongi to eat the first of the New Yam.

When the great day arrives it transforms the intentions of all the principal actors. The secret bargain between Daodu and the Secretary is in disarray. Of the five condemned men due to be reprieved, one has hanged himself in prison and another, Segi's father, has already escaped. Kongi promptly calls off the reprieve and orders that all the condemned be hanged upon the very Day of Harvest. Oba Danlola, hearing as he returns to his palace to dress for the festival that the escaped man is wanted 'dead or alive', resolves that he will not go to swell the pageant of a faithless murderer. Daodu, who has his own ideas about what will really happen at the festival, desperately persuades the king to attend after all.

At the critical moment of the ceremony, Segi's father, returning to attempt the assassination of the dictator, is shot down off stage and killed. But Segi transforms the meaning of his death by presenting his head to Kongi in a covered platter, in the guise of the New Yam. All breaks up in confusion and flight. We leave Danlola and the Secretary at the frontier, their last words suggesting that they are bidding farewell to more than each other. Kongi too, we feel, is probably finished as a political force. The play at least allows us to hope that the future belongs to Daodu and Segi. Daodu's black prayer certainly carries all the impetus of the play's urgency:

> Imprecations then, curses on all inventors of agonies, on all Messiahs of pain and false burdens . . .[1]

The language of *Kongi's Harvest* alternates a fairly racy colloquial prose with passages of verse which make use of arrangements of traditional metaphor to an extent which is quite new in Soyinka, and which may owe something to the example of Duro Ladipo, Obotunde Ijimere and others, whose dramatic texts are largely built up in this way. Here, for example, is the passage in which Danlola conveys his decision

---

[1] *Ibid.*, p. 45.

to attend the New Yam Festival after all:

> DANLOLA: And what Harvest do you children
> Mean to give the world?
> DAODU: Kabiyesi, is it not you elders who say . . . ?
> DANLOLA: The eyes of divination never close
> But whoever boasts Ifa greeted him
> With open lips . . . well, so be it. Sarumi,
> It seems our son will make us mere
> Spectators at our own feast. But
> Who are we to complain? Dada knows
> He cannot wrestle, will he then preach restraint
> To his eager brother?
> SARUMI: Kabiyesi.
> DANLOLA: Well, I will not bear the offering
> Past the entrance to the mosque.
> Only a phony drapes himself in deeper indigo
> Than the son of the deceased.[1]

We may compare this with the way in which Obotunde Ijimere conveys a vital political discussion between the Bale of Apomu and his chiefs in his play *Born With Fire on His Head*. Ijimere began his career as an actor in Yoruba vernacular plays performed by Ladipo's company in Oshogbo. Writing here in English, he makes use of many traditional expressions to trace the argument of justice against expediency which the Bale wages with his chiefs, for the Bale has resolved to punish according to the law the heir to the throne of Oyo, who will shortly have power of life and death over him and his town:

> BALOGUN: When you are chased by a wild elephant
> will you tell him he is trespassing
> on your land?
> OTIN: When Sango strikes your house with fire
> will you say you are innocent? . . .
> BALE: Is my justice to be dictated by fear?
> LISA: Not what is right matters here,
> but what serves our town.

---

[1] *Ibid.*, p. 64.

BALE:	Can a town prosper where crime goes unpunished?
OTIN:	Can a town prosper if it wilfully offends the mighty?
BALE:	Shall I sacrifice my honour and bow to this dissolute youth?
BALOGUN:	Not to him but to Apomu town must you bring this sacrifice.
BALE:	Will you proudly show your head when it shall be said: there goes the Apomu man who dare not do what he thinks is right?
LISA:	I'd rather be laughed at in my house than be respected, sitting on a pile of ashes.[1]

It will be seen how the king and his chiefs stalk one another, always taking care to shelter behind a phrase sanctified by inherited wisdom. Precisely the same effect may be traced in the Yoruba texts of Duro Ladipo, dating from the early 1960's, and this establishes a presumption, at least, that Soyinka has taken note of developments in the contemporary theatre at Oshogbo and elsewhere. Although the use of traditional proverb and imagery can be found in the early plays, he had not previously employed them in such a fashion that they sustain the structure of an entire scene.

Kongi's Harvest is probably flawed as a permanent contribution to the African repertory by its fairly elaborate topicality. Some of the lines will draw less of a laugh even now than in 1965, for certain phrases and attitudes of fashionable dictatorship are already less familiar than they were a few years ago. But a judicious recasting of a line here and there might well serve to revivify the text. Certainly the dramatic form here arrived at, a sort of African political musical with plenty of laughs but a serious and radical tendency, is one which is likely to find imitators up and down the continent. The central line of

---

[1] *Born with Fire on His Head* by Obutunde Ijimere, in *Three Nigerian Plays* (Longmans, 1967), pp. 71–2.

Soyinka's development as a dramatist, however, will probably stem more from *The Road* than from *Kongi's Harvest*, for *The Road* not only develops the system of dramatic ideas present in his earlier tragedies but relates very closely to his parallel achievement in the novel and in his later poetry.

Before turning to examine these, it will be as well to return briefly to the further events of Soyinka's career as a man of the theatre and a public figure. After the proclamation of a State of Emergency in the Western Region in 1962 and the subsequent removal of Chief Awolowo and the Action Group from power, followed soon afterwards by Chief Awolowo's conviction and imprisonment for treason, Soyinka seems to have felt the need for some more immediate weapons of attack than those furnished by the formal drama. The repercussions of the same crisis provoked his resignation, along with many others, from the teaching faculty of the new University of Ife, to which he had recently been appointed. At about this time, also, Soyinka entered upon his second marriage, to his fellow-Nigerian and fellow-teacher Miss Olayide Idowu. The years 1963–5 saw Soyinka increasingly committed to the use of the stage for direct attack upon his political and social targets. For this purpose revue was clearly a better weapon than drama, and it was to revue that he often turned. His talent for this type of writing and presentation rapidly increased his appeal to many who were indifferent to the more searching demands of his plays. His first revue programme, *The Republican*, was staged with the 1960 Masks in February 1964 and played to audiences packed by the very politicians and civil servants who were its principal victims. The cast of this production, which was handled by Yemi Lijadu, included Francesca Pereira, Ralph Okpara and Soyinka himself, the author of nearly all the sketches in the programme.

Encouraged by this success, the 1960 Masks soon revived the production, with a few new sketches, as *The (New) Republican*. This was presented at the Arts Theatre, Ibadan, on 21 March 1964. Although cast and production were largely the same, this programme also 'introduced' a new company, to be called the Orisun Players. Soyinka's idea was to move towards the formation of a permanent, professional acting group which might form the nucleus for Nigerian acting in English, as the companies of Ogunde, Ogunmola and Ladipo had been the nucleus for the professional vernacular theatre. In addition, he wanted a company which, owing to its semi-professional composition, would be a little more secure against the pressure of indignant politicians, for the members of the 1960 Masks were largely in government employ.

Henceforth many of Soyinka's productions were to be billed jointly in the names of both companies, though it was with the 1960 Masks that he directed the first performance of J. P. Clark's tragedy *The Raft* on 9 April 1964, in honour of the state visit of President Senghor. The month of August 1964 saw the most ambitious attempt yet to establish a theatre season in Nigeria which would be something more than one or two-night offerings at the university theatres. Taking the large Obisesan Hall in Ibadan, Soyinka offered there a pro-gramme involving three companies and five different plays on a total of twelve nights within the month. At the same time, he offered a separate production of *Brother Jero* on three nights a week at the Mbari Club. Towards the end of August, a large part of the Obisesan Hall repertoire was offered at the Glover Memorial Hall in Lagos on six successive nights.

This experiment, launched under the title the Orisun Repertory, was unique in other respects besides its scale. It brought together in a single venture and before the same audience the two main streams of development in Nigerian drama. For alongside the English language presentation of *The Lion and the Jewel* by the Orisun Theatre, it offered the ver-nacular plays of the Ogunmola and Ladipo Theatres, the former in *Love of Money* and the operatic version of *The Palm Wine Drinkard*; the latter in *Oba Ko So* and *Oba W'aja*. The whole venture was a clear expression of the joint belief of these three dramatists and theatrical leaders that the time had come to move boldly towards the establishment of a professional theatre which would pass freely between vernacular and

English productions and would strive to develop a joint audience for theatre in the major centres of the country. Companies like Kola Ogunmola's and Duro Ladipo's had been moving rapidly into wider recognition as a result of their appearances on television, at the Arts Theatre and on visits abroad, so that the experiment came just at the right moment to consolidate these developments. Soyinka's part in this venture was rendered easier because he took up no formal post between leaving Ife and joining Lagos University eighteen months later as Senior Lecturer in English.

The next major activity of the Orisun Theatre was another revue, generally judged the most brilliant of all. *Before the Blackout* was played at the Arts Theatre on 11 March and 22–4 April 1965, with an intervening performance on 10 April at the J. K. Randle Memorial Hall in Lagos. Production as well as script was now in the hands of Soyinka himself and there was a significant change in personnel, towards those employed more or less fully in the theatre. These included Betty Okotie, Yewande Akinboh, Wale Ogunyemi, Jimi Solanka and Segun Sofowote. Shortly afterwards a similar cast was to take a new production of *The Lion and The Jewel* to the first International Youth Festival at Nancy, though this was prevented at the last moment by bureaucratic obstruction. This production was directed by Dapo Adelugba, with choreography by Betty Okotie. The latter had now completed her training for full-time professional employment at the Arts Theatre, whilst Adelugba, as lecturer in English and Drama at Ibadan, was also able to devote much of his time to the stage.

During 1965 the situation in Western Nigeria was moving rapidly towards another crisis. A bitterly unpopular government was hanging on to power with increasing difficulty and was generally believed willing to rig the election due in November so as to stay in office. Despite these distractions, the summer of 1965 saw the premieres of two of Soyinka's major plays within a month. On 12 and 13 August the Orisun Theatre and 1960 Masks performed *Kongi's Harvest* at the Federal Palace Hotel in Lagos, where it evoked a tremendous response. This production was directed and designed by Soyinka, with music by Akin Euba. Players who were now increasingly associated with Soyinka's work, several of them being students or employees of the Drama Department and Arts Theatre at Ibadan, filled the principal roles. These included Betty Okotie in the part of Seji and Dapo Adelugba as Daodu. A month later Soyinka was in London for the first performance of *The Road* at the Theatre Royal in the East End of London, where, despite the difficulties of directing such a play with a miscellaneous 'black' cast including West Indians and South Africans, it won a good deal of critical acclaim. This production formed part of the Commonwealth Arts Festival, for which Soyinka also gave a public reading of his new poem 'Idanre'.

He returned to Nigeria almost into the arms of the November crisis. The election being rigged as predicted, Soyinka was accused of indulging in a little freelance political swashbuckling by taping an announcement of an Action Group victory (in a careful imitation of the Premier's squeaky voice) and smuggling it on to the turntable at the Ibadan radio station in place of the official announcement of an 'overwhelming' triumph for Chief Akintola and the N.D.P. This escapade certainly bore the marks of Soyinka's identification of himself as one of 'the strong breed', a writer who cannot hide behind his vocation to avoid direct and personal involvement in events. The accusation landed him in police custody for several weeks and might have led to a prison sentence had the authorities been able to identify him beyond doubt. Among those who believed the accusation, many admired Soyinka's courage; others felt that his concern with the dramatic gesture was likely to expose both him and others to dangers incommensurate with what it might achieve.

Be that as it may, Soyinka was at liberty again by the time of the first coup of 15 January 1966, with whose general objectives he was probably in sympathy. Although the plans of the original coup leaders for forming a purged and unified administration were aborted, Soyinka continued to hope, along with other Southern intellectuals, that some of their aims would still be realized. He had, in particular, a warm regard for Colonel Fajuyi, who was appointed Military Governor of the West. It was in a mood still hopeful and exuberant that Soyinka plunged into preparation of the second production of *Kongi's Harvest*, which had been selected to open the First World Festival of Negro Arts at Dakar on 1 April 1966. This production was mounted at the Arts Theatre, Ibadan, in March and was then transferred to the Daniel Sorano Theatre in Dakar, where construction of the fairly solid expressionistic set Soyinka had designed posed special problems for a theatre apparently unaccustomed to having any sets at all. The reception of this second production was affected by the recent fall of President Nkrumah, which was held by some to give it the air of flogging a dead horse, though it might be argued in reply that dictatorship and its *folies de grandeurs* are very far from dead in Africa. Nevertheless the brilliance and attack of the performance marked a high point in the Festival as an expression of Nigerian theatre before an audience drawn from all over Africa. Much of the excitement of the Festival as a whole was generated by the feeling that Nigeria was blazing new trails in the drama as well as in other branches of literature and the arts.

Returning home filled with legitimate pride in these achievements, the company found itself in the prelude to a crisis that was to do great damage to Nigerian theatre and to the whole cultural life of the nation. In May 1966 came the first wave of violence against Easterners in Northern Nigeria. Soyinka, who happened to be in the North looking for film locations, was profoundly affected by this grim augury of the wrath to come. On 29 July he was at Ikeja when general fighting broke out within the Army, which was to lead to the counter-coup and to the murder, among hundreds of others, of Colonel Fajuyi, who refused to hand over his guest General Ironsi to the mutineers. Hot upon these events came the massacres of September–October 1966 and the steady drift towards estrangement and secession in Eastern Nigeria. Soyinka's horror of war and anarchy must have reached a new peak at this period. Several members of his company, including Ralph Okpara, left for the East and it became daily more evident that the battle lines were forming for a terrible struggle to decide, one way or another, the future of Nigeria. As friends and fellow writers like Chinua Achebe, Christopher Okigbo, Cyprian Ekwensi and Nkem Nwankwo also treked eastwards, Soyinka must have felt a sense of abandonment and helplessness. When news came of secession in Enugu, he is reported to have said, 'They have left us in the lurch.'

4

The Interpreters

1965 was something of a bumper year in Soyinka's output, for it saw the publication of his only novel to date as well as the first performances of *The Road* and *Kongi's Harvest* and the public reading of his major poem 'Idanre'. All these works of 1965 betray a fear of the consequences of the violence which the politicians themselves had so casually invoked for the intimidation of their opponents. All show an awareness of the crass materialism which is eroding traditional values, and the easy-going indulgence with which corruption and inhumanity are commonly regarded. In addition, all except *Kongi's Harvest* show a profound concern for the way in which the gods manifest their will both through human acts and through the contingent moulding of human personality. It is this last concern which lies at the centre of *The Interpreters.*

Writing his first novel, Soyinka broke drastically with the unilinear plots and lone heroes which have hitherto prevailed in African fiction, whether Anglophone or Francophone. To find any work organized with comparable complexity we shall have to look back to Sembène Ousmane's great novel of the Dakar-Niger railway strike, *Les Bouts de Bois de Dieu.* Although the latter is a naturalistic political novel, where Soyinka's is symbolic and mystical, both writers contrive to advance the action through a number of separate figures of more or less equal importance, whose paths only cross or converge occasionally. In Sembène Ousmane's work it is the purpose and situation of the strike which links all his characters and forms the real subject of the novel; in Soyinka's it is the common concern of 'the interpreters' with discovering their own real natures within the total scheme of the great canvas which Kola, one of their number, is painting. His relative inexperience in the art of fiction is revealed in the manner of Soyinka's opening, which requires the reader to assess and relate a number of widely different personalities who are all introduced, without history, in the first few pages of the novel. This helps to explain why a number of readers of this rich and fascinating work have 'given up' after the first fifty pages or so. At this point the mind is congested with partial hints and obscure clues as to what is going forward, but has almost nothing tangible to work upon, either in the form of a discernible plot situated in time or in that of identifiable central characters. It is only the persevering reader who gradually discerns the pattern of self-discovery which discriminates and yet unites the little group of friends as their affairs begin to move towards crisis in the later pages of the novel.

A certain confusion of effect is necessary to Soyinka's purpose, for he wishes to present us with a group of young men and women who are still in the process of clarifying their own identities and finding their place in the Pantheon of gods which forms the subject of Kola's picture. And Kola himself is engaged in the same search, scrutinizing the faces and bodies of his acquaintance for the clues which will finally enable him to fix them in the frozen gesture of paint. But the use of multiple flash-backs, which jump to and fro within the biography of each character, slows up the process of bringing them to any decisive confrontation with one another in anything which we can identify as 'the present'; by which I mean any event clearly following the night-club scene when we first encounter them.

Within a page of that encounter we are already involved in the first flash-back, one which is concerned with the circumstances of Egbo's orphan childhood, his abnegation of the chiefdom which was his by right of birth, and the complex water-symbolism which accompanies or expresses all the great crises of his development. We glimpse already the extent to which the friends might be assisted in their search for self-knowledge by their understanding of one another, but are as yet reluctant to accept the insights thus offered to them. As their characters fly apart again in pursuit of their daily tasks and their own elusive egos it becomes clear that some external catalyst will be necessary to break their self-absorption and bring them into a deeper harmony with one another. In the first part of the novel each seems more intent upon the qualities of his own separation than on any striving for unity or completion within the group, and this itself frustrates the completion of Kola's painting.

Associated with this concentration upon the internal development of each of his characters is Soyinka's tendency to allow each of them in turn to dominate a long passage of the action. Pages 61 to 119,[1] for example, are almost entirely taken up with the affairs of Sagoe, elaborating his twin obsessions with death and excrement until his philosophy of 'Voidancy' threatens to become as tedious to the reader as it is to the hapless messenger Matthias. Just when we have begun to suspect that Egbo, the most 'authorial' of the characters, is going to remain at the centre of the action, this long passage gives rise to a feeling that Sagoe may be taking over this role after all.

In effect, there is no one character in the book who may flatly be proclaimed its hero. In the sense that figuratively he stands always before his canvas, choosing, weighing and placing his fellows, Kola might be thought to occupy this position. On the other hand, the stammering visionary Sekoni, who is killed in a motor accident half-way through the book, may be said to act as the group's pathfinder or pioneer to the frontiers of experience, a role comparable to that of Professor in *The Road*. Sekoni's dream of transforming Nigeria by the modern magic of technology is defeated by the cynicism and corruption of his superiors, but by pouring all his frustrated energy into sculpture he is still able to serve as an inspiration to the friends who survive him. Yet it is Bandele who gradually emerges as the dominant personality of the group, by reason of his very passivity and his quiet insistence upon connecting people with

---

[1] Hardback edition (André Deutsch, London, 1965).

one another, believing that this will most assist their knowledge of themselves. Finally, however, the suspicion remains that it is Egbo who carries the greatest portion of Soyinka's personal concern and identification. For it is Egbo who proves to represent Ogun in the canvas and this god, in his aspect as artist and creative pioneer, has been powerfully attractive to Soyinka ever since *A Dance of the Forests*. None of this guessing is subsequently disproved; it is simply that the centre of the action shifts its position with every change of perspective in the viewer. Soyinka is aiming at 'fulfilment of character'[1] which defies linear time and formal plot-construction.

In retrospect, each of the 'interpreters' may be seen to use one or two key phrases to illuminate his own consciousness. Egbo gives his own 'key' early in the book, when he remarks:

> I suppose I can never wholly escape water, but I do not love things of death.[2]

We have just learnt that his parents were drowned near the Delta town of which his mother was a princess, and that the infant Egbo survived the accident by some apparent miracle. Henceforth all the crises of his life are precipitated by waterscapes. As a boy he would lie for hours in the Oshun Grove at Oshogbo, gazing into the dark, silent waters of the river. But later, he tells us, he learnt to enjoy the river further down where it is spanned by a bridge and runs light and rapid over its rocky bed:

> And there was sunshine. There was depth too in that turbulence, at least I felt down into the darkness from an unfettered sky. It was so different from the grove where depth swamped me; at the bridge it was elusive, you had to pierce it, arrowed like a bird.[3]

We have just learnt of a recent crisis in Egbo's life, the day when he turned aside from the opportunity to succeed his fierce

---

[1] For a full discussion of this concept see Wilson Harris's *Tradition, the Writer and Society* (New Beacon, London, 1967).
[2] *The Interpreters* (André Deutsch, 1965), p. 8.   [3] *Ibid.*, p. 9.

pagan grandfather as king of Osa, the Delta town to which he could have brought the virtues of an enlightened young ruler. It is hard to say whether this was the result of decision or of inanition, for as he sits wavering in mid-stream the adverse tide sweeps his stationary canoe away from Osa and all that it might offer him. What he remembers of Osa is only the charge of a tremendous personal force when his grandfather once gathered him upon his knees and gazed at his supposed heir.

It is also to water that Egbo returns when, exhausted by a night of sensual adventure with his mistress Simi, he clambers upon the rocks in the bed of the swift river Ogun at Ilugun. Again he is beside a bridge, and he stretches himself naked upon the stones, abandoning the Ibadan–Lagos train which goes thundering overhead, in order to encounter a destiny still obscure to him. In the darkness of the night Egbo experiences a sense of sexual[1] possession by the god of the river; he is broken apart and reborn from the husk of his old self. And henceforth he knows himself as the companion of Ogun:

> So now, for the first time since his childhood ascent into the gods' domain, Egbo knew and acknowledged fear, stood stark before his new intrusion. For this was no human habitation, and what was he but a hardly ripened fruit of the species, lately celebrated the freeing of a man . . .
>
> And morning came, baring lodes in rocks, spanning a grid-iron in the distance; it was a rainbow of planed grey steel and rock-spun girders lifting on pillars from the bowels of the earth. Egbo rose and looked around him, bathing and wondering at life, for it seemed to him that he was born again, he felt night now as a womb of the gods and a passage for travellers . . .
>
> And he made it his preserve, a place of pilgrimage.[2]

To this preserve Egbo returns a few weeks later and, upon the altar-stone of his own enlightenment, takes the virginity

---

[1] In a private letter Wole Soyinka has commented: 'I think you are wrong to bring a suggestion of sexual possession into Egbo's experience . . . I distinguish between the mystical and the sexual in religious experience, though I do recognize where the two merge.'

[2] *The Interpreters*, pp. 126–7.

of a young girl whom he is meeting for the first and perhaps the last time. Simi has prepared the way for this consummation, but could not herself be the vessel for it. Yet Simi too is connected with the water imagery which dominates Egbo's development. When he first sees her as a schoolboy in Ibadan, she is interpreted by this imagery:

> She has the eyes of a fish, Egbo murmured, and the boys said, Oh, the creek man has found his Mammy Watta.[1]

And at the very end of the novel, when Egbo is torn between Simi and the scarcely-known girl he took to the river, he senses again that he has escaped one drowning only to succumb to another:

> Egbo watched her [Simi] while she walked towards him, eyes ocean-clams with her peculiar sadness . . . like a choice of a man drowning he was saying . . . only like a choice of drowning.[2]

Though Egbo dislikes 'things of death' he displays a strong vein of violence and a preoccupation with what he calls 'the fact of sacrifice. Ritual immolation'. Thus he immolates the virginity of the young girl and splashes her hymeneal blood upon the rocks. But this act does not purge Egbo of his violence, though he refuses to recognize himself in the 'blood-spattered fiend' depicted by Kola in the Pantheon. Egbo insists upon his identification with 'Ogun of the forge . . . Ogun as the primal artisan', but never with the Ogun who slaughtered his own army in the frenzy of his blood-lust. He will not recognize or accept that, as we have seen in Chapter 2, a vein of destructive violence is inseparable from Ogun's dynamism and creativity, or that this violence can be contained only when its presence has been admitted.

But Kola is right, for Egbo still remains in the role of what the French call the *victimaire*, the one who strikes the blow which kills the sacrifice. It is directly because of his anger at the image

---

[1] *Ibid.*, p. 52. Mammy Watta is a water-spirit of the Niger Delta and the adjoining coasts.
[2] *Ibid.*, p. 251.

of himself in the canvas that Egbo recklessly leaves the young boy Noah alone with the pederast Joe Golder. In the sequel, Golder's inevitable sexual attempt upon Noah leads to the latter's suicide; Noah becomes the unwitting blood-sacrifice to the completion of Kola's painting. And it is again Egbo who strikes the throat of the black ram which is subsequently produced for formal celebration of the work's completion. The passage is highly charged, for Egbo's violent rejection of Golder, whose self-contempt now threatens to overwhelm him completely, has further deepened Bandele's anger against his friend:

> Bandele had said, 'What do you need the ram for? Haven't you had your sacrifice?' And for a long moment, it seemed that Egbo would plunge the knife into his throat and they all stood horrified, round the reek of blood and the convulsive vessel of the severed throat. But Egbo gave the knife a playful flick in his direction and a thin streak of blood marked Bandele across the shirt. Immediately the tension was loosened and laughter replaced the unmeaning moment of antagonism . . .[1]

In these final pages of the novel Soyinka's desire to isolate the deep anger and disappointment of Bandele leads to a certain distortion in the conduct of the others. Noah's death and Golder's guilt are scarcely a day old, but the others have to act with heedless unconcern in order to highlight the moral passion of Bandele and his role as a guide to self-knowledge. For, although the novel does not explicitly state it, Bandele is surely identified with the arch-divinity Orisa-nla or Obatala, the Yoruba god of creation,[2] with his wise passiveness and access to the secret springs of knowledge. In Bandele's case, the key sentence is spoken quite late in the novel, in the more tightly-organized and fast-moving Part II. When the whole group goes to attend an early-morning service at Lazarus's revivalist church on the lagoon, Egbo angrily demands of Bandele what he is getting out of the experience and he replies:

---

[1] *Ibid.*, p. 243.
[2] As distinct from the active 'creativity' embodied in Ogun.

'Knowledge of the new generation of interpreters.'[1]

In the same scene Kola, whose identification of his friends in the Pantheon is largely instinctive, mistakes the boy Noah, Lazarus's latest convert, for the long-sought figure who will unite gods and men in his canvas, as Esumare, the all-embracing rainbow. Explaining why he intends to carry Noah back to his studio at Ibadan, Kola says:

> 'I was thinking of him as Esumare. Intermediary. As the Covenant in fact, the apostate Covenant, the Ambiguous Covenant . . . He does possess that technicolour brand of purity.'[2]

But Kola has mistaken the nature of Noah's apostasy. His real affinity is with the slave Atowoda, who treacherously rolled a great boulder upon the head of the arch-divinity Orisa-nla and smashed him into the thousand fragments through which man must now worship him. When Kola and Egbo return to the now flooded lagoon church to fetch Noah, they find him being subjected to a kind of ordeal by fire. Burning oil has surrounded the church and through this fire comes Lazarus to rescue his chosen Apostle, but Noah flees in terror from an ordeal which Lazarus (whom we have earlier seen calmly watching a fire-swallowing performance at a night-club) endures unflinching. It is this scene which causes the reader, as well as Kola, to reassess Lazarus. For it is Lazarus who proves to be the catalyst that will precipitate a new knowledge of one another among the interpreters. His methods do not differ greatly from those of any other charlatan revivalist of the Brother Jeroboam variety, but it may be that his claim to have risen from the dead is both literally bogus and imaginatively true. Or, to put it otherwise, it does not greatly matter whether it is true or not. What matters is that Lazarus now proves to be the figure who can unite Kola's canvas and express the divine Covenant of rainbow and multi-coloured boa, 'the vomit-streak of the heavenly serpent'. It is as such that Kola finally paints him, at the very

[1] *Ibid.*, p. 178. [2] *Ibid.*, p. 178.

moment when the rejected Noah proves his acceptability for another role, that of the inarticulate sacrifice who dies that others may progress towards self-knowledge. Through this sacrifice it may be that even the odious Joe Golder will eventually find redemption. Golder is a destroyer, as we learn from his confession that he has already driven his own father to suicide.[1] But Kola finds room for him too in the canvas, as the animal-god Erinle, and Egbo certainly attracts blame for his refusal to include the broken Golder within the scope of his compassion. For Golder too is an artist, one who dares disintegration in order that he may find completion.

The way to Kola's final integration of his vision has been prepared by Sekoni, who blurts out at one point:

'In the dome of the cosmos, there is complete unity of Life. Life is like the godhead, the plurality of its manifestations is only an illusion. The godhead is one. So is life, or death; both are contained in the single dome of existence.'[2]

In the same way, Sekoni's brief and inspired career as a sculptor has given Kola the necessary impulse to complete his painting. Sekoni is in these senses *ahead* of the other interpreters, but it is perhaps his very haste towards enlightenment that precipitates his own death on the slippery darkness of the road. And this death itself precipitates his friends' tentative movement towards self-fulfilment in the last pages of the novel.

Finally there is Sagoe, with his twin obsessions of death and excrement. The juvenile aspect of his character should not blind us to his integrity, or to the fact that these are very rational obsessions for anyone inhabiting a city like Lagos. He brings them into a single focus in the important scene where he first encounters Lazarus, at the funeral of an Apostle:

A battered car—it looked like a nineteen forty-five Vauxhall— moved so slowly that the two immediate followers often

---

[1] *Ibid.*, p. 188.
[2] *Ibid.*, p. 122. (I have eliminated the original indications of stammering. *Ed.*)

knocked their shins on the rear bumper. It was the greatest farce ever enacted before death. For the car was moving with an open boot and the turd which stuck out so disgustingly was the coffin. The procession was—he had an urge to count them—a mere eleven. They were clumsy and their grief seemed true.[1]

Sagoe is, in his own ribald fashion, also a pathfinder, since it is his encounter with Lazarus which precipitates the events that bring the novel to a climax. He is purged in the fire of his long duel with Dehinwa, who witholds the love she contains so abundantly until he is ready to receive it.

In an interesting paper[2] Professor Eldred Jones has shown the importance of taste as an indicator of true civilization in *The Interpreters*. Whereas the inner group of friends all possess a certain artistic sensibility, characters like Chief Winsala, Sir Derinola and Professor Ogwuazor reveal their lack of spiritual grace in the tawdry objects and borrowed rituals with which they surround their lives. It would be a mistake, however, to suppose that Soyinka is showing us a world composed of a few elect and a great army of the damned. Both Noah and Lazarus, for example, find their place in Kola's scheme of things. Though Dehinwa's bad taste is emphasized, she plays a vital role in Sagoe's slow progress to maturity. Likewise, Simi helps Egbo to recognize the nature and demands of his own sensuality, whilst Monica Faseyi teaches Kola his need of love. Are these, then, not also interpreters in their fashion? The principal butts of Soyinka's satire may be left at the end of the novel without a glimpse of redemption, but the machinery for their redemption is there, only awaiting recognition. That satire is, however, occasionally crude and even brutal. The lawyer Lasunwon, who often accompanies the friends on their night-club expeditions, appears to have no function other than to register his own insensitivity to nuance and atmosphere.

---

[1] *Ibid.*, p. 111.
[2] 'Progress and Civilization in the Work of Wole Soyinka', read at Ife University, December 1968.

Monica Faseyi's fearless stand for informality occasionally seems merely perverse, as when she refuses champagne at a party and demands palm-wine. Both are excellent drinks and they do not invite comparisons of moral value.

There is some dross, then, in *The Interpreters*, and the novel might have benefited from a more stringent revision. But what remains is a work of extraordinary complexity, richness and interest. If Soyinka attempts too much, he has also accepted the challenge of bringing his tragic vision of African life within the compass of a novel. He has resisted the temptation to put all his moral eggs in the basket of a single hero and has instead offered us a group of characters whose social freedom, sincerity and serious talent embody the creative vitality always as evident in Nigeria as the tendency towards chaos and disintegration.

5

Later Poetry and *Idanre*

One of Soyinka's last acts before his arrest in August 1967 was to visit London and check the final proofs of his first volume of poetry. When *Idanre* appeared in the autumn of that year it was found to contain none of the poems with which his early reputation as a satirical poet was established. Not only did he omit such immature works as 'The Immigrant', 'The Other Immigrant' and 'My Next Door Neighbour', but even the accomplished 'Telephone Conversation' was laid aside, perhaps because he felt it was in danger of becoming his anthology piece. Equally surprising was the omission of his early tragic sequence 'Requiem', in which many of the ideas explored in his later poetry and plays first appear. Here already is that vividly realized sense of the physical reality and process of death; its involvement with the very substance and rhythm of life; its insistence upon being heard, upon making known the world which surrounds our existence:

> Now, your blood-drops are
> My sadness in the haze of day
> And the sad dew at dawn, fragile
> Dew-braiding rivulets in hair-roots where
> Desires storm. Sad, sad
> Your feather-tear running in clefts between
> Thorned buttresses, soon gone, my need
> Must drink it all. Be then as
> The dry sad air, and I may yield me
> As the rain.[1]

---

[1] *Modern Poetry from Africa*, ed. Moore and Beier (Penguin, 1963), p. 114.

Instead of issuing a random collection of poems written over the previous decade, Soyinka has produced a highly-organized work in which only the short poem 'Luo Plains' has the look of an occasional piece. The effect is to emphasize once again that consistency in his ruling ideas and images which has been demonstrated throughout the present work.

The first group of poems reverts to the theme of the road, image not only of sudden death but of the terrible cost exacted by technical progress in Africa. The road points not only towards the future but towards the past, and movement along it can be in either direction. This ambiguity in the potentialities of the road had been remarked upon already by Joyce Cary in *Mister Johnson*:

> The road itself seems to speak to him. 'I'm smashing up the old Fada—I shall change everything and everybody in it. I am abolishing the old ways, the old ideas, the old law; I am bringing wealth and opportunity for good as well as vice, new powers to men and therefore new conflicts. I am the revolution ... I destroy and I make new. What are you going to do about it; I am your idea. You made me so I suppose you know.
>
> Rudbeck, staring at the road, feels rather than understands this question and he feels again a sense of confusion and frustration. It seems to him, not to his reason, but to his feelings, that he has been used and driven like a blind instrument. This gives him a very disagreeable sensation. He stands for several minutes smoking and gazing, with a kind of disgusted surprise, and then gives a snort so loud that a passing headman bobs a curtsey and says in a mildly apologetic tone. '*Zaki*'.[1]

Cary is much more of a symbolist in his novels than is commonly realized and the road, with its ever-mounting toll of deaths and injuries, is a fairly obvious symbol for the Moloch of human progress. But Soyinka is able to add to these universal associations of the road those more specific ones which depend upon its links in Western Nigeria with the cult of Ogun, god of exploration and artistic skill, but god also of war and all its

---

[1] *Mister Johnson* (Michael Joseph, 1939), pp. 168–9.

insense slaughter. Thus the polarity of Ogun's nature matches that of the road, and yet another plane of reference is added by Soyinka's own identification with Ogun; an identification which, as shown by the *Interpreters*, includes an equal aware-ness of the polarity between creativity and violence in the poet's character. All these planes of reference are present in a poem like 'Death in the Dawn', where the presage of the white cock's impalement upon the speeding car is not recognized until the poet comes upon the dead man clenched in the embrace of death; only then do both deaths relate themselves as images of what awaits everyone who ventures unwarily upon road:

> Traveller you must set forth
> At dawn
> I promise marvels of the holy hour
> Presages as the white cock's flapped
> Perverse impalement—as who would dare
> The wrathful wings of man's Progression ...
> But such another Wraith! Brother,
> Silenced in the startled hug of
> Your invention—is this mocked grimace
> This closed contortion—I?[1]

The brilliant precision of some of the images in this poem is likely to be appreciated fully only by those who have travelled the roads of West Africa in the hour before dawn, feeling for themselves 'The dog-nose wetness of the earth' and glimpsing the apparently gaunt figures of the women striding with their great head-loads:

> in faceless throng
> To wake the silent markets—swift, mute
> Processions on grey byways ...[2]

Another poem in this group laments the early death of Segun Awolowo, son of the Nigerian politician, who was the victim of yet another senseless road-smash. Here too move the ideas which were to be fashioned into the very framework of *The*

---

[1] 'Death in the Dawn'. *Idanre* (Methuen, 1967), p. 10.   [2] *Ibid.*

Road. The churning lorries of Nigeria are seen as terrible reapers who glean no proper harvest, but fill the morgue-granaries with the stacked bodies of the young and urgent. For those who fall so suddenly and out of season there can be no instant rest:

> In sounds as of the river's
> Failing pulse, of shifting earth
> They make complaint
>
> Grey presences of head and hands
> Who wander still
> Adrift from understanding.[1]

In the studies of loneliness which follow, Soyinka finds a paleness in the colour of a tropical Easter which matches our own fear of suffering:

> Do we not truly fear to bleed? We hunt
> Pale tissues of the palm, fingers groping
> Ever cautious on the crown.[2]

And the question prepares us for the pains and losses of the third section, 'of birth and death', whose tone is set by the grim vision of 'Abiku', by poems lamenting a still-birth and a child lost on its 'first deathday', and by another which lends monumental grandeur to the stretched forms in a mortuary.

'Abiku', written at least eight years ago, is still one of Soyinka's most powerful poems. Unlike J. P. Clark, who makes a moving appeal to the compassion of an Abiku (literally 'child-born-to-die', a spirit-child which torments the mother by its constant cycle of birth and infant death), Soyinka sees it as a creature of an alien world, utterly beyond our anger or our pity. The opening lines strike already the note of chill mockery in Abiku's observation of our rituals:

> In vain your bangles cast
> Charmed circles at my feet

---

[1] 'In Memory of Segun Awolowo', *Ibid*., p. 15.

[2] 'Easter', *Ibid*., p. 21.

I am Abiku, calling for the first
And the repeated time

Must I weep for goats and cowries
For palm oil and the sprinkled ash?[1]

Balefully, Abiku watches the futile attempts to earth his limbs
in the planting of yams and taunts the living with their practice
of branding the dead spirit-child before burial, that it may be
known again upon return. Likewise, the pouring of libations
only points the child towards the 'understreams' whence it
came. Abiku, though he appears a child, is truly ageless and forever apart, hostile or at best indifferent to our endeavours. Even
the warmth of the womb is cloying to him; even an egg-yolk,
universal symbol of generation, is only material for the shaping
of burial-mounds.

In this bleak poem, Abiku turns to mockery the very rituals
through which Soyinka later suggests growth, promise and
fruition in his tender 'Dedication' for the birth of his daughter
Moremi:

> ... plumb her deep for life
> As this yam, wholly earthed, yet a living tuber
> To the warmth of waters, earthed as springs
> As roots of baobab, as the hearth.[2]

Here peppers, kernels, palm-oil, wine and honey all serve to
swell the form and prospects of the blessed child, preparing
her for the ringing dedication of the last lines:

> ... haste to repay
> The debt of birth. Yield man-tides like the sea
> And ebbing, leaving meaning on the fossilled sands.[3]

Lighter in mood, too, is Soyinka's polemical astonishment over
his first white hairs, springing unbidden amid his 'Hirsute hell
chimney-spouts'. But the sombre mood returns in 'Post
Mortem', at the end of this same section, balancing the images

---

[1] 'Abiku', *Ibid.*, pp. 28–9.   [2] 'Dedication', *Ibid.*, p. 24
[3] 'Dedication', *Ibid.*, p. 25.

of birth with those of death. A body stretched under the surgeon's knife suggests to the living poet that discipline and a kind of grandeur may be sought in the contemplation of greyness. Here it is perhaps the twilight world between sleeping and waking, between lapsing and emerging states of consciousness, that is suggested by this evenness of palette—for is not the brain upon the surgeon's scales also grey?

> let us love all things of grey; grey slabs
> grey scalpel, one grey sleep and form,
> grey images.[1]

This poem prepares us for the exploration of nature's greyness in the section entitled 'grey seasons'. Here too there is a predominance of all that is bare, hard and enduring. The heavy rods of a tropical downpour teach 'purity of sadness' as they beat unrelentingly upon the earth. Even the colours of a harvest scene suggest only rust and decay while the mental treadmill of imprisonment is imagined by one who was later to experience much of it himself. The last lines of 'Prisoner' close with authority one of Soyinka's most sustained and deeply-felt poems:

> . . . He knew only
> Sudden seizure. And time conquest
> Bound him helpless to each grey essence.
> Nothing remained if pains and longings
> Once, once set the walls; sadness
> Closed him, rootless, lacking cause.[2]

In these poems there is a sense of energy closed upon itself, circling like a pool lashed by rain among the rocks. Yet when release of that energy comes, as it does in the following section, 'October '66', it brings only horror and dismay. All that enables Soyinka to write these difficult and honest poems is his ever-frustrated hope of better things, of harvest fructified by the unmeasured sacrifice of today. For now the full frenzy

---

[1] 'Post Mortem', *Ibid.*, p. 31. [2] 'Prisoner', *Ibid.*, p. 44.

whose first motions he had glimpsed in May has been unleashed. The methodical slaughter of 29 July 1966, when hundreds upon hundreds of Ibo officers, soldiers and civilians perished, has been followed by an undiscriminating hurricane of death in the Northern Region. Leaving the country for a few weeks soon afterwards, Soyinka looks back on these events and draws them into some kind of utterance. In 'Harvest of Hate' he compares them to what should have been at this season of national renewal:

> There has been such a crop in time of growing
> Such tuneless noises when we longed for sighs
> Alone of petals, for muted swell of wine-buds
> In August rains, and singing in green spaces.[1]

But in 'Massacre', it is the imagery presented to him by a European autumn through which alone he is able to handle the unseasonal death that has fallen upon his land. Swimming in the lake at Tegel, he can comprehend events from which he has 'briefly fled' only by seeing them through the screen of falling blood-red leaves and the pale autumn sunshine that surround him:

> A host of acorns fell, silent
> As they are silenced all, whose laughter
> Rose from such indifferent paths, oh God
> They are not strangers all
> Whose desecration mocks the word
> Of peace—*salaam aleikun*—not strangers any
> Brain of thousands pressed asleep to pig fodder—
> . . .
> I borrow seasons of an alien land
> In brotherhood of ill, pride of race around me
> Strewn in sunlit shards. I borrow alien lands
> To stay the season of a mind.[2]

Here once again there is an astonishing correlation between

---

[1] 'Harvest of Hate', *Ibid.*, p. 50.

[2] 'Massacre, October '66', *Ibid.*, p. 52.

Soyinka's preparation for his craft and the tasks presented to him as a poet. Long and solitary brooding upon the processes of physical dissolution and renewal, upon the processes of spiritual energy, upon plenty and its price, upon the disciplining of language towards what is hard and strong, have given the poet the imaginative equipment to convey his anguish and compassion without loss of control. In the poem 'Civilian and Soldier', which records his encounter with an armed man at the very height of the Ikeja fighting in July, he even manages a dry humour. Contrasting the soldier's trade of death with his own trade of living, he scorns the hesitation in the performance of his martial role that made the soldier spare him. If their places are ever reversed, Soyinka will hesitate not at all, but will shoot the soldier 'clean and fair' with all the good things of life that are now menaced by his weapons and his incomprehension.

This deeply impressive group of poems of 1966 is marred only by the inclusion of one which displays Soyinka's occasional tendency towards an excessive violence of expression. 'Malediction' is presumably addressed to a woman who rejoiced (as many, alas, did) at the hideous deeds committed in these months. Such rejoicing certainly deserves scorn and anger, but does it merit this?

> thin slit in spittle silting
> and bile-blown tongue
> pain plagued, a mock man plug
> wedged in waste womb-ways
> a slime slug slewed in sewage ...[1]

Here the energy of Soyinka's response has betrayed him into an excess of hatred as ugly as the emotion he attacks. The result is bad poetry.

To forge a union of destructive energy of this kind and the creative force of art is the central preoccupation of his only long poem to date, 'Idanre'. Set among the great elephant-coloured boulders of the Idanre mountain, this poem inter-

---

[1] 'Malediction', *Ibid.*, p. 55.

weaves the legend of Ogun's ancient violence with memories of Soyinka's own ascent of the mountain and with a future vision of Sango and Ogun in creative union. Legend recounts how the inhabitants of Ire once persuaded the demi-urge Ogun to descend from his self-imposed retirement and serve them in war against their neighbours. Reluctantly he descended to this task but, his blood-frenzy once aroused in battle, fell upon his own army as well as the enemy and slaughtered them almost to a man. The energy of Sango, god of lightning and thunder, is likewise destructive in much of its expression, though often interpreted by men as divine vengeance. Soyinka dreams in this poem of Ogun playing among the great cables of modern electricity (which represent the harnessed power of Sango), so that his skilful hands may shape the land anew. After all, the iron *asen* (staffs) of Ogun which are planted in the earth of his shrines—and outside Soyinka's own house at Ibadan—often catch and conduct the terrible energy of Sango in precisely this fashion. Once within the womb of earth, such energy will be released in harvest:

> And no one speaks of secrets in this land
> Only, that the skin be bared to welcome rain
> And earth prepare, that seeds may swell
> And roots take flesh within her, and men
> Walk naked into harvest-tide.[1]

In 'The Fourth Stage' Soyinka discusses the significance of the role played by iron in Ogun's original plunge into the gulf of transition. It was with material drawn from the fertile womb of earth (iron) that Ogun protected himself from the peril of disintegration during his journey.

Thus the final emphasis of the poem is not upon ancient violence, minatory though it is on that subject, but upon the promise of fulfilment that informs the rain-drenched morning as the poet descends the mountain and takes wine from the hands of the girl who is also Oya, divine wife of Sango:

---

[1] 'Idanre', *Ibid.*, p. 82.

. . . He who had dire reaped
And in wrong season, bade the forests swallow him

And left mankind to harvest. At pilgrim lodge
The wine-girl kept lone vigil, fused still
In her hour of charity

A down of bright processions, the sun peacocked
Loud, a new mint of coins . . . [1]

Ogun has withdrawn once more to the dark forests of Idantre, charging his servant, the artist, with the task of regeneration. The last reverberations of storm and tempest have died away, leaving the air of morning quiet and expectant. So Ogun's road is finally seen as a 'Möbius' strip, thus:

the tail-devouring snake which has ever stood as mankind's symbol of perpetual regeneration, and which is frequently hung around the necks of Ogun's worshippers.

Throughout this collection, Soyinka exhibits a poetic style which is vocal rather than visual. Even his lyrics show less

---

[1] *Ibid.*, p. 84.

concern with pattern upon the page, with metrical regularity, or with rhyme, than with 'breath'. It is those quasi-dramatic changes of tempo and of emphasis, so clearly indicated in the writing, which give to these works the formal discipline of poetry. Unlike many African poets writing in English, Soyinka can handle both a long line and a long paragraph with assurance. His most persistent weakness, not wholly purged even in 'Idanre', is a tendency to overload his lines, creating an effect of strain and turgidity:

> Who, inhesion of disparate senses, of matter
> Thought, entities and motions, who sleep-walk
> Incensed in Nirvana—a code of Passage
> And the Night—who, cloyed, a mote in homogeneous gel
> Touch the living and the dead?[1]

Here there is little sense that a question is being asked, for the question fails to articulate the involved and wandering movement of the stanza.

A poem of 1966 like 'Civilian and Soldier', on the other hand, displays a perfect control of movement, a control which holds the tragic and comic components of its irony in equipoise. In general, the development of Soyinka's poetry towards a profound seriousness of tone has been accompanied by increasing mastery of his highly distinctive language.

Idanre was published within a few weeks of Soyinka's arrest and is, with the exception of his vigorous English version of Fagunwa's *Ogboju Ode Ninu Igbo Irunmale*,[2] the latest major work we have from his pen. Although not prolific as a lyrical poet, he has shown in this volume a great deepening as well as darkening of his art. The progress from 'Requiem' to 'Post Mortem', or from 'Telephone Conversation' to 'Civilian and Soldier', is that from a brilliant colonial student to a mature poet measuring the tragic weight of the present hour. Lovers alike of literature and of human liberty have waited his return to activity with impatience.

---

[1] 'Idanre', *Ibid.*, p. 62.
[2] Translated as *The Forest of a Thousand Daemons* (Nelson, 1968).

Conclusion

In the early summer of 1967 Soyinka was appointed head of the Drama Department and the Arts Theatre at Ibadan University. This was a logical and welcome development for all who wished to see Nigeria's outstanding dramatic talent in control of the institution most likely to establish a professional repertory company and train its personnel. A few weeks later, before he was even able to take up the post, Soyinka appears to have got drawn into an active role in the political effort to avert civil war in Nigeria. The exact circumstances of this are not yet known and are best left without comment for the moment. What is certain is that Soyinka was arrested in mid-August 1967 and was held in detention and largely *incommunicado* for over two years. The consequences for theatre development in Nigeria were serious and prolonged, though happily he has now been able to take up his appointment and return to full activity.

In the spring of 1969, while still in prison, he was able to send two short poems[1] to a friend in London, poems which bear the authentic stamp of his courage and humour. 'Live Burial' comments on his own entombment:

> Sixteen paces
> By twenty-three. They hold
> Siege against humanity
> And Truth
> Employing time to drill through to his sanity

and closes with a characteristic ironic gesture:

> Bulletin:
> He sleeps well, eats

---

[1] *Poems from Prison* (London, Rex Collings, 1969)

Well. His doctors note
No damage
Our plastic surgeons tend his public image.

The other poem, 'Flowers for my Land', takes a sad reckoning of all that is lost. It ends with a call for the lighting of sun-beacons on every darkened shore of the world. But looking nearer home, Soyinka does not see the stir of new life in the carnage which these years have wrought, and his own flame of hope burns low:

Death alike
We sow. Succeeding horror
Whets inhuman apetites
I do not
Dare to think these bones will bloom
tomorrow

The necessity for this kind of painful witness was foreseen by Soyinka in two important papers, 'And after the Narcissist?', published in 1966 and 'The Writer in the Modern African State',[1] which he read to a literary conference at Stockholm in February 1967. In the first, he attacks the self-absorbed, incantatory mode which seems to him to prevail in African literature and to divert its attention from contemporary social reality:

Narcissism begins when the writer fails to distinguish between self-exploration and self-manipulation ... the true African sensibility [is that] in which the animist knowledge of the objects of ritual is one with ritualism, in which the physical has not been split from the psychic, nor can the concept exist of the separation of action from poetry. Music is not separated from the dance, nor sound from essence. Incantatory poetry cannot signify more than the prelude.[2]

The second paper is a call to precisely this kind of action.

---

[1] Published in *The Writer in Modern Africa* (Uppsala, Scandinavian Institute of African Studies, 1968).

[2] *African Forum*, New York, Vol. 1, No. 4, Spring 1966.

Soyinka points out that in colonial Africa, the writer who got into trouble with authority might be sustained by the sympathy of his own people; in the run-up to independence he might swim with the tide of popular emotion; but in the sober light of today he must learn to rate truth above the pleasures of easy company and public approval. Decrying the tendency of many black writers to take refuge in a flattering and insulating mythology of African innocence, he declared:

> It seems to me that the time has now come when the African writer must have the courage to determine what alone can be salvaged from the recurrent cycle of human stupidity.

These words embody the whole tendency of Soyinka's own endeavour over the past decade and no fitter ones could be found for ending this short study of his achievement.

Selected Bibliography

PLAYS

Three Plays
(The Swamp Dwellers, The Trials of Brother Jero, The Strong Breed)
Book design and illustration by Denis Williams, Mbari Publications, Ibadan, 1963.

The Lion and the Jewel
Oxford University Press, London and Ibadan, 1963.

A Dance of the Forests
Oxford University Press, London and Ibadan, 1963.

Five Plays
(A Dance of the Forests, The Lion and the Jewel, The Swamp Dwellers, The Trials of Brother Jero, The Strong Breed).
Oxford University Press, London and Ibadan, 1964.

The Road
Oxford University Press, London and Ibadan, 1965.

Kongi's Harvest
Oxford University Press, London and Ibadan, 1967.

POETRY

Three poems in *Black Orpheus* 5, Ibadan, May 1959.

'Two in London' (The Immigrant, . . . And the Other Immigrant) in *An African Treasury* edited by Langston Hughes, Crown Publishers Inc., New York, 1960.

Eight poems in *Modern Poetry from Africa*, edited by G. Moore and U. Beier, Penguin Books, London, 1963 & 1968.

Idanre
Methuen, London, 1967.

Poems from Prison
Rex Collings, London, 1969.

FICTION

The Interpreters
André Deutsch, London, 1965.

The Forest of a Thousand Daemons
(Translated from D. O. Fagunwa), Nelson, London, 1968.

CRITICAL WRITING

'Towards a True African Theatre', *Transition* 8, Kampala, March 1963.

'And After the Narcissist?', *African Forum*, New York, Vol. 1 No. 4, Spring 1966.

'The Writer in An African State', *Transition* 31, Kampala, June 1967, (reprinted in *The Writer in Modern Africa*, Scandinavian Institute of African Studies, African Publishing Corp., New York, 1969).

'The Fourth Stage', in *The Morality of Art*, essays presented to G. Wilson Knight, edited by D. W. Jefferson, London, Routledge and Kegan Paul, 1969.

Index

A

B

M

Malediction, poem by Wole Soyinka, 92

Massacre, poem by Wole Soyinka, 91

Mister Johnson, novel by Joyce Cary, 86

Modisane, Bloke, South African writer and actor, 7

The (New) Republican, revue presented by *The 1960 Masks* at the Arts Theatre, Ibadan, 1964, 68

The 1960 Masks, Soyinka's first acting company, 15; production of *Song of a Goat*, 44; *The 'New' Republican* revue, 68; first performance of *The Raft* by J. P. Clark, 69; first performance of *Kongi's Harvest* at Lagos, 1965, 70

N

Nkrumah, President, 64, 72

Nwankwo, Nkem, Nigerian author, 5, 73

Nwoke, Demas, Nigerian artist, 29

O

Oba Koso and *Oba W'aja*, vernacular plays of the Lapido Theatre, 69

Ogun, Yoruba god of iron, war and craftsmanship, 4, 12, 31, 32, 35, 39, 40, 41, 42, 45, 54, 55, 56, 63, 77, 78, 79; Soyinka's identification with, 86–7; 93, 94; ceremonies at Ishede and Ilodo in southeast Dahomey, 11–12

Ogunde, Hubert, founder of a Theatre Party in 1945, 61

Ogunmola, Kola—director of a Nigerian musical and dramatic group, 61

Ogunyemi, Wale, Nigerian actor, 70

Okigbo, Christopher, Nigerian poet, 5, 73

Okotie, Betty, Nigerian actress, 45, 70, 71

Okpara, Ralph, Nigerian actor, 29, 43, 68, 72

Olusola, Segun, Nigerian actor, 44

Orisa-nla or Obatala, Yoruba god of creation, 80, 81

The Orisun Players formed by Wole Soyinka in 1964, 68; repertory season of the Orisun Theatre, 1964, 69; *Before the Blackout*, revue, 1965, 70; first performance with *The 1960 Masks* of *Kongi's Harvest*, 70

S